HAMPSHIRE

Edited by Kelly Oliver

First published in Great Britain in 2003 by
YOUNG WRITERS
Remus House,
Coltsfoot Drive,
Peterborough, PE2 9JX
Telephone (01733) 890066

SB ISBN 1 84460 232 X

FOREWORD

Young Writers was established in 1991 as a foundation for promoting the reading and writing of poetry amongst children and young adults. Today it continues this quest and proceeds to nurture and guide the writing talents of today's youth.

From this year's competition Young Writers is proud to present a showcase of the best poetic talent from across the UK. Each hand-picked poem has been carefully chosen from over 66,000 'Hullabaloo!' entries to be published in this, our eleventh primary school series.

This year in particular we have been wholeheartedly impressed with the quality of entries received. The thought, effort, imagination and hard work put into each poem impressed us all and once again the task of editing was a difficult but enjoyable experience.

We hope you are as pleased as we are with the final selection and that you and your family will continue to be entertained with *Hullabaloo! Hampshire* for many years to come.

CONTENTS

Joseph Borzych (11)	18
Lucy Ysselmuiden (10)	19
Michael Chalmers (9)	19
Katie Roe (11)	20
Charlie Beardsmore (11)	21
Michael Whelan (10)	22
Kieran Child (10)	23
Tiffany Francis (11)	24
Emma Wilson (10)	24
Camilla Rogers (10)	25
Michael Harris (11)	26
Emma Cox (11)	27
Oli Knowles (10)	28
Hannah Neat (9)	29
Emily Moss (9)	30
Matthew Pocock (9)	30
Olivia de Courcy (10)	31
Ally Spong (10)	32
Katie Strick (9)	33
Charlie Pullen (9)	34
Rebecca Crouch (9)	35
Roy Alderton (10)	35
Katrina Duncan (10)	36

Meon Junior School

James Butler (10)	36
Alexander James Herrington (11)	37
John Chang Liu (10)	37
Connor Hayes (11)	38

Micheldever Primary School

Peter Ballard (10)	38
Magnus Barber (10)	39
Zara Yeates (10)	39
Simon Foot (10)	40
Joanna Bassett (9)	41
Hannah Cozens (11)	41
Christie Emmerson (11)	42

Guy Meager (8)	59
Beth Graham (9)	59
Jessica Hobbs (9)	60
Hannah Rodgers (9)	60
Rhiannon Thomas (8)	60
Thea Arnott (7)	61
Jessica Evans (7)	62
Abigail Joy Singleton (9)	62
Jessica Humm (8)	63
Lizzie Flesher (8)	63
William Cook (7)	63
Claire Stratton (7)	64
Kirsten Adams (7)	64
Josh Wade (8)	65
Simon Hunt (9)	65
Catherine Gisborne (9)	66
George Harris (9)	66
Claire Bogan (8)	66
Faye Buckle (9)	67
Elizabeth Pinniger (9)	67

St Peter's RC Primary School, Winchester

Max Tinkler (9)	67
Philippa Falconer (9)	68
Jeneba Brewah (9)	68
Ben Dexter (10)	68
Bethany Harrison (9)	69
Shana Woodbridge (10)	69
Charlotte Poffley (9)	69
Emily Rogers (10)	70
Nicholas Sommer	70
Danny Foy (9)	70
Toby Coen (10)	71
Monique Martin (9)	71
Nicholas Kidd (10)	71
Jordan Dempsey (10)	72
Luke Duff (9)	72
Bethan Steane (10)	72

Erika Hoffman (10)	73
Claire Mills (10)	73
Lydia Ricketts (10)	73
George Tutton (11)	74
Danielle Stainer (11)	74
Emma Buckett (9)	75
Almariza Menton (10)	75
David McHardy (10)	76
James Mahood (11)	76
Lynne Moreto (11)	77
Luke Kingshott-Taylor (10)	77
Francesca Wild (11)	78
Kate Eastham (10)	78
James Fenton (10)	79
Bethany Rose (9)	79
Lauren Sanders (9)	79
Elise West (10)	80
James Kearney (10)	80
Mary Barlow (10)	81
Katy Palmer (11)	82
Valerija Custance (11)	82
Zoë Morgan (10)	83
Karim Kazane (11)	83
Rosie Clayden (10)	84
May Sawyer (9)	84
Lizzie Underwood (11)	85
David McKenna (9)	85
Isabel Ronaldson (10)	86
Jack McCabe (9)	86
Caitlin O'Kelly (9)	87
Stephanie High (10)	87
Lily Stead (9)	88
Jade Coward (10)	88
Joe Lewis (11)	89
Duncan Bray (11)	89
Alex Gambrill (10)	90
Aicha Zaa (11)	90
Katherine Nahajski (10)	91

James Thorpe (11)	92
Barbara Speed (11)	92
Rosie Fagan (10)	93
Hillie Nouwens (9)	93
Claire Whitfield (10)	94
Mary Sims-Howlett (10)	94
Amelia Thomson (10)	94
Georgina Falconer (11)	95
Ellen Culhane (11)	95
Isla Dixon (10)	96

Somerton Middle School

Jake Kelly & Shannon Wootton (9)	96
Katie Williamson & Sophie Bull (9)	96
Lucy Morris & Sarah Tuckwell (9)	97
Megan Crews & Jordan Ayton (9)	97
Chelsea Harrison (9)	97
Elizabeth Kelly & Emily Dale (10)	98
Molly Burnip (9)	98
Kathryn Bunker (9) & Annabel Randall (10)	99

The Grey House School

Alexandra Moore (8)	99
Louise Ingham (8)	100
Cameron Gaul (7)	100
Alex Bruce (8)	101
Philippa Gleadow (10)	101
Jemima Ridley (10)	102
Andrew Rankin (8)	102
Alice Rudland (7)	103
Jonathan Manson (8)	103
Georgia Pike (11)	104
Emily Fearon (9)	104
Tara Kirby (8)	105
William Long (8)	105
Tom Coussins (10)	106
Chloe Young (9)	106
Krishan Pujara (10)	107

Westbourne Primary School

Whitewater CE Primary School

The Poems

SOMETHING ABOUT MY TEACHER

She walks in, silence surrounding the atmosphere.
She steps closer and closer towards *you!*
She can hear your knees clatter against each other in total silence.
She calls herself Mrs Blood; she feeds off children's fear.

You are in her class, seems as every minute passes, you are getting
                                                            older and older.
You start work on witches, wondering if she's one.
You finish her class with relief, but one catch, she gave us homework.
You start to walk, suddenly she calls you over, you slowly turn . . .

She towers over you, smelling your fear
She tells you that you were rude for talking in class
She says that she will see you later, literally
She starts to puzzle you, wondering what she means

You slowly come into Tutor, hoping she isn't there
You sit down quietly, then a shadow forms over the desk
You peer up, seeing her there, just standing over you
You go home saying, 'It keeps on going and going.'

Zach Crabb (12) & Beth Crabb (11)

LOVE

Love is red, as red as blood
Love is like a flower bud
Love is all around the world
Love reaches every girl and boy
Love is when we give love presents
Love is when Valentine's day comes
On Valentine's day we send love to friends
Love is having girlfriends.

Tim Chambers (10)
Four Marks CE Primary School

LOVE

Love is red, love is kind,
Let us help those who are blind.

Inside your tummy, love feels all funny,
When love comes everyday, it is sunny.

Love is so romantic,
People love to sail on the Atlantic.

When you see your boyfriend,
You always like to get a card to send.

Love is fun, love is sweet,
People just can't stay sitting in their seat.

Love is so cute,
Boys sometimes like to wear a suit.

Lisa Keywood (9)
Four Marks CE Primary School

LOVE

Love can sometimes make you dizzy
and also it can be quite squidgy.

Love can make your tummy feel funny
and also like a pile of money.

Love makes you make cards in the shed
and then you can get wed.

Boy and girl make a good pair,
that's why people stand and stare.

Holly Smith (9)
Four Marks CE Primary School

LOVE

Love is true
Love is good

Love is you
That's what love is

On the bench
In the park

Your insides sing
Like a skylark

In the air
Love lingers

People stare
At love

And then . . .

Natasha Oakes-Monger (9)
Four Marks CE Primary School

LOVE

Love is like a rainbow with so many different colours,
Love is bright red, to make your heart have flutters.

Love is sometimes blue, when you are sad,
Love is yellow, when you are mad.

Love is green when you just lost your only desire, your only cost
And that's when you start to cry
About your secret that will never die.

Hannah Lacey (9)
Four Marks CE Primary School

VALENTINE'S DAY

Love is gentle
And kind too
I have love
And so do you

Love is everywhere
And should be too
So please be kind
'Cause love is true

Love is honest
Plus rosy red
Love passes through you
Until you are dead

So please be gentle,
Honest and kind
Your family will
Always be in your mind.

Amy Kerslake (9)
Four Marks CE Primary School

LOVE

Love is nice and very red,
You make secret cards in your shed.

Sometimes you can get quite shy,
You're embarrassed, so you tell a lie.

You chase the girls around the playground,
Until your girlfriend has been kissed and found.

Victor Anderfelt (8)
Four Marks CE Primary School

LOVE

Love is good, love is true,
out in the world, your true love is waiting for you.

Love is heart-warming and all red,
make secret love letters under your bed.

Boyfriends, girlfriends, family too,
you love them and they love you.

Love is fantastic, love is fun,
go on holiday in the Mediterranean sun.

Eleanor Saunders (8)
Four Marks CE Primary School

TEN THINGS FOUND IN A GARDENER'S POCKET

A rusty rake,
Seven sunflower seeds,
A bag of soggy soil,
A big, pretty plant pot,
A roll of grated grass,
A very loved, but old, spade,
A wonderful water feature,
A big hosepipe,
A wet watering can
And
A tatty trowel.

Aimée Walker (10)
Four Marks CE Primary School

TEN THINGS I FOUND IN A DOCTOR'S POCKET

I found ten things in my doctor's pocket . . .

An old rusty stethoscope
A stainless steel surgeon's knife
One hundred and one patient's phone numbers
A bottle with a greeny-red liquid inside
A 'How To Be A Surgeon' pocket book
An extremely heavy hammer
An old trainee name tag
Two halves to an amputation saw!
A bottle labelled 'urine sample' (it was full!)
Seven, 30 foot long bandages!

Samuel Chapman (10)
Four Marks CE Primary School

TEN THINGS FOUND IN A WITCH'S POCKET

Five forgetful frogs,
The icky ingredients for making boys,
(Slugs, snails and puppy dog tails),
A black cat,
A five foot broomstick,
The lovely ingredients for girls,
(Sugar, spice and everything nice),
Ten poisonous toadstools,
Some infected eyeballs
And one wonderful wand.

Imogen Wood (10)
Four Marks CE Primary School

THE BIG MATCH

The players are getting ready,
As it gets closer to the match,
The manager is talking about tactics,
As the keeper's practising his catch.

The whistle blows for kick-off,
Man U get it under way,
Roy Keane takes a serious fall,
The ref has to stop the play.

Roy Keane has to go off,
Nicky Butt takes his place,
David Beckham takes the free kick,
The ball goes at an almighty pace.

It hurtles into the back of the net,
Man U go 1-0 up,
The Arsenal fans are in despair,
They're going out of the cup.

The first half has ended,
The players leave the pitch,
Roy Keane is still being treated,
With plasters and a stitch.

The second half goes quickly,
There are two more goals,
The people who scored them are,
Ryan Giggs and Paul Scholes.

The game is all over,
Man United have won,
The trial for cup glory,
Has finally begun.

Joshua Collins (10)
Four Marks CE Primary School

THE BIG PIG RACE

There was squealing and grunting
And twitching of tails,
As the six little porkers all took their place.
There was Trotter and Hammy, Little Pink Pig,
Peggy and Tammy and Spot.
They lined up together in anticipation,
The race was about to begin.
The crowd started cheering as the farmer arrived,
Waving the green flag to start.
They're off! They're off!
The crowd shout with joy,
Which one is going to win?
Hammy's in front, next is Peggy, then Spot,
The others are close behind.
The crowd is full of excitement
As Spot goes into the lead.
The finishing line gets nearer and nearer
As Spot is running so fast.
The farmer smiles proudly,
While watching his little pigs run.
The race is nearly over.
The crowd are cheering loudly as . . .
Little Pink Pig beats Spot to first place!

Melissa Rose (11)
Four Marks CE Primary School

THE RACE

They all said the hare would win,
But for some reason, tortoise entered in,
They were both raring to go,
When the starter fired his gun,
Both hare and tortoise began to run.

Hare sprinted ahead,
Then decided he would go to bed.
He snuggled down on the road,
But tortoise kept slowly plodding along,
While whistling an old folk song.

Tortoise increased the dawdling pace,
While hare rolled back on his furry face,
Tortoise had a cheeky smile
And could see the finish line
Next to an old evergreen pine.

Hare was still fast asleep,
On the road, in a heap.
Hare's snoring just got louder,
Tortoise was so close,
He really wanted to boast.

Hare suddenly heard the bellowing crowd,
Their cries really very loud,
He woke up with a shock,
His legs running,
Heart really pumping.

He was just two yards clear,
But tortoise very near,
Tortoise passed the important tape,
Winning excellent first place,
Including the medal in a shiny case.

Jenni Beckwith (10)
Four Marks CE Primary School

TIM THE STUPID BOY

Tim was a stupid boy
He wasn't very clever,
Didn't work at all hard
And did well in tests, never.

Tim was sick of being bullied
He was sick of being shamed,
Because he was so stupid
He always got the blame.

So at school he listened carefully
As school he studied well,
His SATs results
You just couldn't tell.

So on the day of the SATs
He filled in all the tests
And Tim the stupid boy
Did better than all the rest.

Thomas Paul (11)
Four Marks CE Primary School

HE SUCCEEDS

As Arthur crosses the ribboned line,
He can't believe he's done it,
All he can hear is the packed crowd's cheer
And it's all he can do not to vomit.

He goes to get his ribbon,
Finally it's a red!
The teachers say, 'Oh well done!'
I really want my bed!

Abi Robinson (10)
Four Marks CE Primary School

MY BROTHER

My brother's name is Christopher,
He's only eight years old,
He's very good at football,
Especially scoring goals.

And if he's not playing football,
He's always watching telly,
Or else he is in the cupboard,
Looking to fill his belly.

At seven o'clock in the evening,
He isn't very full,
So be aware to be raided,
By Christopher! He's cool!

Charlotte Kirk (10)
Four Marks CE Primary School

TEN THINGS FOUND IN A GARDENER'S POCKET

A rake that is razor-sharp.
A collection of slimy slugs, ready for Sunday lunch.
A bag of seeds ready to be sown.
A lawnmower cutting the long grass.
A handful of soil, damp, dark, dirty, sticky soil.
A pitchfork as sharp as a shark's jaw.
A tub of slug pellets ready to be sprayed.
A fork as sharp as a blade.
A handful of worms, fighting in the grass.
A shovel, ready to dig in the yucky soil.

Beau Cleveland Copeman (9)
Four Marks CE Primary School

THE END OF THE JUNGLE

Down in the depths of the jungle
All of the animals tussled,
They heaved and pushed and fought
Using their massive muscles.

They fought for eternity and longer,
Just fighting, clawing day and night,
They never realised what they'd done,
Until they finally saw the light.

The fearless eagle screeched,
The fierce lion roared,
The monkeys all climbed up their trees
And even the sloth didn't snore.

For the end of the jungle was coming
And every beast knew why,
For all of the animals fought
And now they were all going to die.

The end of the jungle came
Quicker than light I expect,
But every animal was reborn
And showed each other respect.

James Locke-Scobie (11)
Four Marks CE Primary School

MRS CASE

Our Secretary, Mrs Case,
Wears bangles that are in their place.
She answers the phone,
With a very loud ring tone,
She wears shoes that you tie with a lace.

Josie Livingston (10)
Four Marks CE Primary School

A SWIMMING GALA

My gala was, of all types,
An invitation meet
And there I swam my heart out,
I couldn't stay on my feet.

I posted in my card
And took my seat on a chair,
I felt like a bucket of lard,
But I just didn't care.

They seemed to be too good,
That put me in all of a flutter,
But upon the blocks I stood,
Feeling like a nutter.

My dive was a thing of beauty
And my arms rotated so fast,
You didn't have time to dawdle,
If you would see me as I passed.

My tumbleturn had speed,
As my instructor later said,
On my wild stampede,
Nothing could stop my lead.

I touched the wall at last,
Which put me in first place,
I must say I enjoyed,
My 50 metre race.

As I went up to collect my medal,
My trophy and shield too,
I had my mind on the race
And what I'd managed to do.

James Whitehead (10)
Four Marks CE Primary School

SCHOOL DINNERS

It makes Mrs Fowler grumpy,
That the custard is cold and lumpy;
The meat is ever so chewy
And is very, very gooey,
The jelly is as solid as a rock
And the soup has a mixed-in sock,
The meatballs are hard, round and plumpy!

Sophie Blackman (9)
Four Marks CE Primary School

HEAVEN

Heaven is as clear as glass,
As smooth as glass,
As reflective as glass.
Break it, stop believing, and bad luck forever.
In Heaven everyone has their space,
Their time.
You can be whoever you want.
Heaven is like a candle
Shining through the night.
Blow it out, dampen its spirits,
You'll walk in darkness.
When it's lit, it'll point to Heaven.
Turn it upside down, it will not change.
Ever faithful light.

Elina Mann (10)
John Keble Primary School

HEAVEN

As I look at the road to Heaven,
My heart shudders,
My hands shake and I don't know what to do.
Should I walk into paradise?
It feels like I've been cut in half,
One side of me wants to but the other doesn't.

Lara Weston (10)
John Keble Primary School

MRS TUMBLE

'No chewing gum Bob.
Do your laces up Kate.
Andrew, no whispering.'
These are the things that Mrs Tumble hates.
'What's that you've got Tim?
Take it outside!
I want you all to listen
Make your ears wide.
I told you no whispering,
Stand in the corner.
Your name's on the board,
Make sure it gets no longer.
No pointing Jim!
Don't laugh at the back.
I have had enough of you lot and
I will never come back!'

Charlotte Murphy (10)
Langrish Primary School

THERE I STOOD IN THE MOONLIT SKY

There I stood in the moonlit sky,
Waiting for a shooting star to go by.
The moon peeping in the trees,
Baby squirrels sleeping peacefully.

There I stood in the moonlit sky
Looking at a gleaming star go by,
The birds singing in the trees,
As the moon slowly flows on its way.

There I stood in the moonlit sky,
I'm flying in the yellow clouds.
As the moon dies down
And drifts off across the cool air.

Kirsty Mudkins (10)
Langrish Primary School

SHADOWFAX

Charging through the land of trees,
Clad in white from mane to knees.
His eyes are free of guilt and fear
He finds his master but doesn't rear.

Two more come but these are brown,
They reach their leader and bow down.
Yet they are surely not the best
They'll soon have to lie and rest.

Their master moves onto a path,
He's old, withered and holds a staff.
He mounts the white steed fondly,
Shadowfax that horse is he.

Jack Spooner (11)
Langrish Primary School

UNTITLED

A ferocious cat paws the sand,
Slowly creeping towards the land.
Here she prowls and up she preys
Hurtling boats across her bays.

Her slick tongue licks up sand and stones,
Her wind it blows, howls and moans.
A streamlined wave, swallows the sky,
She jumps to catch it, way up high.

Revenge of sun visits at morn',
The bright light awakens crack of dawn.
An eerie shadow covers the creek,
A boat anchor slowly begins to grow weak.

Her purring batters long lost ships,
Drifting, diving, down it dips.
Their sails flutter, west to east,
Her wind is like a vicious beast.

Dusk arrives, a calming friend,
A wailing song his colours send.
Flaming orange and relaxing red,
Slows the cat to the under seabed.

Emma Foster (11)
Langrish Primary School

PIZZA

Now pizza is that kind of thing,
Which is made to be the shape of a ring.
Olives, ham, cheese and all
Makes a cake look like a fool.

You can buy them in restaurants, cafés as well
And they don't give off a horrible smell.
Tomatoes, juicy, the ham is fresh,
Now the pizza's at its best.

The melted cheese on top,
Is enough to make you *pop*.
I asked ten people and what did they say?
'We'll have a pizza any day!'

Matthew Salmon (11)
Langrish Primary School

WINTER

The hedges used to hide the birds,
Now they are as bare as anything.
All the trees are brown and naked,
Thick fog, like a blanket over the hills and mountains,
Butser Hill - you cannot see.

Farmers are moving their herds
Into their barns to keep warm.
Flowers' scent you can no longer smell,
Sparrows, robins, thrushes and crows
Hunting to keep themselves alive.

Joseph Borzych (11)
Langrish Primary School

BREAKFAST

I like breakfast, I like lunch
But at school, there's no time for brunch.
Breakfast; eggs, bacon and ham,
Sometimes even cheese and jam.
Potato waffles, mushy peas,
Mango juice, freshly squeezed.
Juicy grapefruit on a plate.
Mushrooms and onions are the foods I hate,
Pancake coated in sugar and lemon
Have you tried them with melon?
Coco Pops drowning in creamy milk
Thick white yoghurt looks like silk,
Sizzling sausages in the pan,
Fried eggs from the milkman.
Now I've had breakfast, it's time for lunch.

Lucy Ysselmuiden (10)
Langrish Primary School

MOVE!

'Get out of the way, squirt!' James moaned.
'Why?' Rachel asked.
'Because I want a drink!'
'Why?' she asked again.
'Because I'm thirsty!'
'Why?' she asked for the third time.
'Because I haven't had a drink all day!'
'Why?' she asked for the fourth time now.
'Because I am forgetful!'
'Why?' she continued.
'Because I get it from Mum!' James replied.
'Mum, James called you forgetful!'

Michael Chalmers (9)
Langrish Primary School

WALK THE PLANK

As the great mass hovers way up high,
Clouds of mist gather in the sky.
Creatures gaze at an amazing sight,
Standing out in the great bold light.

The captain steers from the right to left,
Sailing away from his latest theft.
The ship's giant mast, pierces the clouds,
The crew sings joyfully, very loud.

Birds cannot fly far above,
We cannot hear the *coo* of the dove.
The wind blows fast around me,
In the pitch-black, I truly can't see.

The fog steams up the small portholes,
I stare enviously at the gleaming gold.
Bobbing along, I felt seasick,
I know now all was a mischievous trick.

As a dagger is pointed at my throat,
I realise that I am leaving the boat.
I am forced on to the edge of the plank,
The sky before me is completely blank,
I prepare to fall to the ground again!

Katie Roe (11)
Langrish Primary School

CLOUDRIDER

I'm soaring through the evening sky,
Wisps of cloud are floating by.
The sun above is bright and true,
The sea below is clear and blue.

Swiftly diving round and round,
Up to the sky, then down to the ground.
Flitting around, so wild and free
Obstructions simply turn and flee.

Far below a fish does leap,
My amber eye spots the meat.
I start to dive, I need the food
Let the fish prepare to be chewed!

The glint in my eyeball, the wind in my wings,
The sound of the waves seems to sing.
Tearing, speeding, racing the air,
I won't release my daily fare.

Suddenly the fish ducks down,
I can't reach it, it's out of bounds.
I can't pull out, I'm going to crash,
And so I did, into the great mass.

The pain in my wing is unbearable,
I lost my snack, it's unbelievable!
I lie in the water like shark bait,
And then, quite suddenly, I awake.

Lying soundly in my bed,
No pain in my arm but my face is red.
Downstairs, the cat made a *purr*
It made me realise I'm not a bird.

Charlie Beardsmore (11)
Langrish Primary School

WAR

War, why war?
For blood and gore?

War, why war?
For blood and gore?
To kill good Christian men!

War, why war?
For blood and gore?
To kill good Christian men!
To waste fresh people's lives?

War, why war?
For blood and gore?
To kill good Christian men!
To waste fresh people's lives?
We must defeat the bad, the evil of this world,
But war, why war?

No war! Just *remember*
God gave us life
God gave us youth,
God gave us the world
So don't waste it on war.

Michael Whelan (10)
Langrish Primary School

THE EDGE

Sanctaphrax tall and round,
Undertown, below its ground
As waterfall round and round.

Danger lurks in the twilight woods,
To keep strangers out for good.

Deadly moles roam the mire,
As the professor works in the tallest spire.

The healing waters of Riverrise,
To the howling Deepwood cries.

The Edge River rolling down,
Passing flight rocks round.
Never to return to the stable ground.

I read the story flicking through the pages,
As the flight rock engages
And the fire rages.
I finish the book, my brain blazing,
I can't put it down, it's too amazing.

Kieran Child (10)
Langrish Primary School

THE EAGLE

Way up high above the mountain tops,
I soar like a plane, searching for prey,
I scan the Earth, way, way down below,
A movement startles me and off I go.

Tearing down, through the blue, cloudless sky,
Wind rushes through my wings, as I glide.
Other birds stare at me as I swoop,
Upside-down, sideways and loop-the-loop.

Finally, I break to a hover
And keep my eagle eye, out for prey,
A palomino shrew scrabbles, scared,
I swoop - he's gone and I take him away . . .

Tiffany Francis (11)
Langrish Primary School

THE METAL HORSE

The metal horse
With its steel legs,
Silver-plated mane
Its iron head.

The metal horse
With its aluminium tail.
Its rigid skin
Its metallic hoof.

The metal horse
With its stiff bronze ears,
Its tin tongue
Its small lead teeth.

Emma Wilson (10)
Langrish Primary School

THE GREY MARE

As she canters here and there,
Her mind asks, 'What, how, when, where?'
She's trapped in a pasture,
And galloping faster,
She looks like she's seen a bear.

Her flickering bloodshot eyes,
As blue as the northern skies,
They're darting around,
Her hooves hit the ground,
By men, she is despised.

The men will chase and shout,
She's turning inside out.
They are just so mean
It's like her worst dream.
But she still gets daily clouts.

All of the men have trapped her,
You could say that it's a capture.
She's trotting quite fast,
It's not going to last.
No, she couldn't have snapped the . . .
. . . gate!

Camilla Rogers (10)
Langrish Primary School

THE ANIMAL

It was there that I saw it,
With its concentrated eyes lit,
It takes one step, then one step more,
Just before pounding across the forest floor.
It has seen something small and round,
Its small, young paws, makes no sound.

It chases the rabbit through the wood,
And within its heart, contained no good.
The fat, round rabbit, struggles for life,
But the creature's claws cut through it like a knife.
The rabbit's gone, its hunger quenched,
It starts for home, slowly getting drenched.

Its grumbling stomach no longer asks,
As it passes through the forests many green masks.
It enters the area containing its lodge,
Whilst avoiding the places it has to dodge,
It walks slowly back towards its den,
It stops outside and greets its ten.

Michael Harris (11)
Langrish Primary School

WHY ARE YOU LATE FOR SCHOOL?

Why are you late for school?
I'm late Sir because I couldn't get up
And I couldn't get up
Because I was weary,
And I was weary
Because I went to bed late,
And I went to bed late,
Because I had a detention,
And I had a detention
Because I wasn't paying attention,
And I wasn't paying attention
Because I was staring out the window
And I was staring out the window
Because I saw a plane drift through a cloud.
I'm late Sir, because I saw a plane drift through a cloud!

Emma Cox (11)
Langrish Primary School

THE DRAGON OF FIRE

The sun rises behind the hill,
Lighting the mountain of rock
And perched up high you see him -
The dragon of fire.

Down below in a field of grass
An intruder has stolen some sheep,
But no ordinary intruder is this -
The dragon of ice.

Back on the hill, he sharpens his eyes
Now he's enraged, he takes to the skies
And begins to circle his rival -
The dragon of fire.

He takes to the air, prey in his claws
But when he sees the other
He drops the lamb to the ground -
The dragon of ice.

Flames wander up the throat,
Eyes begin to flicker.
Then out it comes in one great blast,
The dragon of fire.

With his powers lost
He struggles to fly, his strength fading.
His body falls and rests on the grave,
The dragon of ice has fallen!

Oli Knowles (10)
Langrish Primary School

WHAT AM I?

As I leap and jump in the air
I twist and twirl, landing in the sea's lair,
My graceful body seems to fly
Watched closely by passers-by.

As I swim in the sea,
Everyone watches me.
So I bow-ride by the boat,
It's as if I'm afloat.

Diving deep for fish,
I find a shoal - that I miss.
When I look out of my eye,
A predator I spy.

As he comes up to me
I jump and flee.
I escape through a reef,
Seaweed seems like a leaf.
What am I? A dolphin.

Hannah Neat (9)
Langrish Primary School

THE HORSE

Galloping, galloping over the plains
Galloping, galloping fast as a train.
Over the hillside, over the field,
Under the canopy hanging over the old shield.

The wind in my hair, the wind in my face,
Blowing beside me like it is a race.
I'd run a bit faster, then run a bit more,
Until I reached the stable door.

I'd zoom around it, I'd gallop on,
I'd keep going while the sun shone.
Then I'd settle down for a drink
An quietly rest on a steep brink.

Emily Moss (9)
Langrish Primary School

THE ALIEN

The alien walks at night
His antenna wiggles and whirls,
When you watch it, you'll get a fright,
When you stare at it, your hair swirls.

He's all purple and red
From his tentacles and his beady eye
And he also lives in my garden shed,
But oh look at him fly!

He climbs out of his cramped ship
And into the dark and gloomy dusk.
He will walk away and get back on his ship
And fly away to a far away land.

Matthew Pocock (9)
Langrish Primary School

THE OLD OAK TREE

There's an old oak tree
At the bottom of our playground,
It has a very boring life, it seems
Just standing there, day and night.
No one knows how old it is,
Just standing there, through the mist,
In other weathers too.
Rain, shine, hail, snow and frost - almost anything.
It can't do what we can do,
Just standing there all the time.
All the branches twisted round,
None of them do touch the ground.
The old oak tree at the bottom of our playground,
Is very beautiful, especially in springtime.
But all it does is stand there
And it always will do, forever!

Olivia de Courcy (10)
Langrish Primary School

I SAW A STRANGER I KNOW

I saw a stranger on my holiday
On the plane and coach.
Renting out some skis
And on the slopes again!
On the chair and bucket lift
And in the shop again!

I saw the stranger at the lake,
Catching fish, big and small.
I saw him getting money at the fish stall
And I saw him on some scales.
I turned around but no one was there,
I realised something silly -
Now the truth I didn't know is
That the stranger is *me!*

Ally Spong (10)
Langrish Primary School

IF PIGS COULD FLY

If pigs could fly,
Then I would too.
For I'd love to sail through the sky so blue
And plane, bird or passer-by
Would never ask, 'What is the time?'
For high above, up there too -
A great main clock
Is the sun, so huge!

If pigs could fly
Birds would not,
They'd laze in mud and get very hot.
They wouldn't go *chirp* but they would go *moo,*
And eat banana's like a monkey too.
They'd wear raincoats
And wear wellies as well.
How they would look, I really can't tell!

Katie Strick (9)
Langrish Primary School

THE WINTER

I love winter, I love the feel of it,
The taste of it, the smell of it.
I love winter so much,
When frost and snow is on the ground.
I love winter.

I love the style of winter,
The way all the roads and paths make people skid.
The winter tales people tell to make children shiver.
I love winter.

I love the feel of winter,
When the cold air comes along.
Swishing my face like a grizzly bear
The cold chilly feeling of winter.
I love the winter.

Charlie Pullen (9)
Langrish Primary School

A COLD NIGHT

A cold night, a horse went riding by:
But was it a horse or a cold white ghost?
Cold white ghost it was! It was!
What was it?

A cold night, a car went whizzing by:
But was it a car or a black coffin?
Black coffin it was! It was!
What was it?

A cold night, a rabbit went running by;
But was it a rabbit or a big green monster?
Big grey monster. It was! It was!
What could it be?

Rebecca Crouch (9)
Langrish Primary School

POEMS ARE HARD

Poems are hard
I never get it right,
When I write this poem
I'll stay up all night!

Well if this poem
Is very good,
I'll be happy,
I would if I could.

Actually this poem
Isn't making me feel queasy
It actually seems -
Quite easy!

Roy Alderton (10)
Langrish Primary School

A WOODLAND WALK

As I scuff my feet over dry autumn leaves,
I see something yellow, it looks like a bee.

A little grey squirrel, picking up nuts
And with one bite, the nut he cracks.

Some trees sway from side to side,
There's a bird, he likes to glide.

A prickly hedgehog shuffling by
And a twittering sparrow that catches my eye.

Thud! I fall in a rabbit hole,
Oh look! There's a little black mole.

As I walk back out of the wood,
I say 'I like nature, I think it's good!'

Katrina Duncan (10)
Langrish Primary School

FLYING

I wish I could fly with the wings of a bird,
Flying above all, soaring over the many streams of cold
Invigorating air, encircling me.

I wish I could soar above the stars in the sky,
Swoop down over an archipelago of islands,
Placed in the deep blue water.

I wish I could view the rise and the set of the sun,
The bright yellow and oranges in the beginning
And the deep red streaks in the end.

James Butler (10)
Meon Junior School

GOD TALK

God is a myth,
Made up by humans.
I don't know why
They did that!
No one is in control,
Who did that?
If God didn't do this . . .
Who did?
God is a myth,
Made up by humans.
What happened?
Why do they feel like
Someone is in control?
God is also an
Aeroplane crashing
Into buildings!
Is He lightning?

Alexander James Herrington (11)
Meon Junior School

GOD TALK

God is a myth - thought of and not thought of.
Some say He is a figure of our imagination.
Some say He is a Father to us all.
God is as huge as a 200 storey building,
God is as busy as an aeroplane in August.
He is a being of kindness and love,
He guides people to do good deeds.
We never see, hear, feel or smell Him
But some people think He's everywhere.

John Chang Liu (10)
Meon Junior School

GOD TALK

God lives in a world of peace,
But He also lives in us.
He makes the wind blow and the leaves on trees rustle,
He can make the flowers bloom and
The grass swish along the ground,
But He can also make it Heaven.

In a matter of hours, He can make
Something very dreadful.
A tornado!
This dreadful beast can rip trees off their roots,
It rips houses apart until there's nothing left,
Except a crisp packet
Lying on a bedroom floor.

Connor Hayes (11)
Meon Junior School

TRUCKING DISASTER!

The truck came down the track
Taking Tango to Twyford.
It came to a halt
With a bump and jolt,
Losing a nut and bolt.
They got the tool box
Where there were lots of spare nuts and bolts
So they put on a nut and bolt,
Then they were back on the track
Trucking away in their truck.
They got to Twyford and
Found they had lost all their Tango.
What a trucking disaster!

Peter Ballard (10)
Micheldever Primary School

MY BEST FRIEND

He wears no jumper at all,
He is the acronym of small.
He is good at maths
And likes taking baths
And now and again, has a brain!

He is my very best mate,
But at breaking-up he's great!
He is learning how to handstand
To be the best in the land
And when he comes round, I can't wait!

He never ever thinks up a con
Even though his Grandma has gone!
He tends to be bad
But never gets mad
My special friend is Simon.

Magnus Barber (10)
Micheldever Primary School

HULLABALOO

H ere is my poem for Hullabaloo,
U nless you don't like it,
L ucky for you.
L ong or short, it's up to me,
A crostic, riddle or verse, that's free.
B ack to the start or maybe not,
A ttacking my head, my brain is too hot.
L ook at this poem,
O h, help me please.
O h, I'll never complete it, so I'll always be teased.

Zara Yeates (10)
Micheldever Primary School

ABC FOOD

A is for apples, small and crunchy,
B is for buns, full of sugar,
C is for cream, sitting on apple crumble,
D is for Doritos, triangular shaped crisps,
E is for eclairs, covered in chocolate
F is for French bread, which comes from France,
G is for gammon, poor little pig.
H is for ham which goes in sandwiches,
I is for ice cream, cold in my tum,
J is for jam, goes on my toast.
K is for kiwi which comes from down under!
L is for lamb, best mate - a roast spud.
M is for milkshake, I get in Burger King,
N is for nuts - I use a nutcracker.
O is for orange, not colour,
P is for peas, somethings I hate.
Q is for quiche, I like it a lot
R is for raisins, a kind of dried fruit
S is for soup, you have for starter,
T is for tomatoes, very juicy.
U is for ugly fruit, something sweet
V is for veal, a baby cow,
W is for water, plain but nice,
X is for *x-tra* pudding, I have it a lot.
Y is for yoghurt which comes in a tub,
Z is for zabaglione, a kind of fruit.

Simon Foot (10)
Micheldever Primary School

WHAT LIES BENEATH

I walk amongst the many trees,
Gently treading on soft green leaves.
Then I find beneath the grass
A little door of battered brass.
I open it and as it creaks,
A world of wonder within I peek.

A voice echoes, 'Come in, come closer, closer . . .'

I go along at a steady stroll,
Then something emerges from my soul.
'I am your soul-mate, your mind and heart,
When you betray, we slowly part.'

Joanna Bassett (9)
Micheldever Primary School

THE FAMILY RACE

Your family is immovable,
Their love is a shield.
You're the centre of their world,
They would do anything for you.

You're a part of a team,
That wins the race,
Of kindness and happiness,
That's all it takes!

Hannah Cozens (11)
Micheldever Primary School

THE BLACK SHADOW

It waits, listening,
Crouching silently,
Eyes are sharp,
Whiskers twitching,
Suddenly
Ears prick up,
A noise is heard.

It pauses,
Quickly locating its target
It slowly rises,
Then moves swiftly,
Slyly creeps
Tail swishing,
Senses alert.

Once close,
It freezes.
Choosing the moment,
Preparing to pounce.
It springs,
Teeth bared -
Ready to tear at the victim's throat.

Then silence,
The kill is over.
With its stomach full
The jaguar leaves.
Just a shadow -
Gone!

Christie Emmerson (11)
Micheldever Primary School

MY BROTHER

My brother paints and
Stays in his room,
Drew some pictures,
He fights a lot.
He shouts out loud
And plays football
And he likes chips.
He plays UNO
But he ignores me.
He plays with Tyne Class
At home he plays with Connor and Callam.
Goes on the PlayStation and computer.
He sleeps quietly,
But he takes the covers off me.

Samantha Hide (10)
Micheldever Primary School

SILENCE

Grassy mounds surrounded by tulips,
A carpet of bluebells haunted by souls.
Dull grey death markers, bearing gifts from loved ones,
Snowdrops clumped together in pure white patches,
A thin dirt path leading up to the great stone dwelling
With its stained glass window, capturing the light
And the Holy altar -
Silence!

Abigail Watton (10)
Micheldever Primary School

THE BIG, BIG POEM

In the big, big universe, there was a big, big world,
And in the big, big world was a big, big country.
As there was a big, big country, there was a big, big town,
So in the big, big town, there was a big, big house.
In the big, big house, there was a big, big room,
But in the big, big room, was a big, big cupboard.
Suprisingly, in the big, big cupboard, there was a big, big box,
And in the big, big box was a big, big monster.
Suddenly the big, big monster gave a big, big *'Boo!'*
As all big, big monsters do.

Matthew Mackenzie (10)
Micheldever Primary School

THE SNAIL

Slow, steadily plodding along
The snail is getting hungry,
Slow, steadily crawling along,
The snail is very near.
Slow, steadily lolling along
The snail reaches its goal.
Slow, steadily sliding along
The snail is full of lettuce.
Slow, steadily eating away.
The snail is now asleep.
Zzzzzz!

Antonia Wyatt (9)
Micheldever Primary School

WHATIF ... ?

(Based on the poem 'Whatif' by Shel Silverstein)

Last night whilst I was in my bed
some whatif's came into my head.
I was fed up all night long
because the whatif's sang an annoying song.

Whatif I party all night?
Whatif I die by a blinding light?
Whatif I climb up a tree?
Whatif I get stung by a bee?
Whatif I break a delicate pot?
Whatif I get into trouble a lot?
Whatif I have to do a dare?
Whatif I get eaten by a bear?
Whatif I have to carry a baby?
Whatif I have to go crazy?
Whatif I get bit by a terrible mouse?
Whatif I fall in love with a sport?
Whatif I get a really big wart?
Whatif I run out of *whatif's?*

Amanda McCulloch (10)
Micheldever Primary School

ICE

Ice sparkles like a ruby in the sun.
It reflects the gleaming sun's rays
Onto the delicate and fragile snow.
Ice spreads all over the country
Like a thick sheet of velvet.
It thickens and sets on the water
Like a jelly in the fridge.

Edward Holland (9)
Potley Hill Primary School

THE SEA SONG

Along the sandy seashore, especially in a storm,
You can hear a noise, like a distant bee swarm.
But even though, it's a strange shivery sound,
You can feel it quiver and shake, the sound
Weaving through the ground.

Along the rotting jetty, even on a sunny day,
You can hear an unusual creaking
Which makes you want to stay.
But even though it's a wind-waving branch sound,
You can feel it creak, crack, shivering,
Shivering through the ground.

That's the sea song,
Playing all night long,
Even on a sunny or stormy day.

Helen Walker (9)
Potley Hill Primary School

NO NAN!

Nan, Nan, oh don't say that Nan!
It's really not cool,
What will people say when I go to school?
Nan, Nan, don't wear that!
Nobody wears woolly hats!
Nan, Nan, do we have to listen to the
Brotherhood Of Man?
You really must be their only fan.
Nan, Nan, you may not be as cool
As you could be,
But I know you'll always be there for me!

Laura Marsden Payne (8)
Potley Hill Primary School

THE LOVELY QUEEN

Off she goes
In a carriage pulled by white horses,
Wearing a dress
Maybe a suit.
A beautiful crown with sparkling jewels.

That's my idea of
The lovely queen.

She lives in her glittering palace
Her gardens so big and green
With flowers gleaming with pleasure
And her majestic trees swaying in the wind.

That's my idea of
The lovely queen.

Francesca McWade (9)
Potley Hill Primary School

SNOW

As white and soft as cotton wool,
As silent as a snake spying its prey.
Hills of whiteness filling the sky,
Snowmen standing in the cold wind.
Building up mounds of cold white mud.
Crunching like crisp packets as you step,
Thick layers of white icing on branches of the trees.
Waters turn into layers of stone,
Melts in my hand as I pick it up.

Spencer Shaw (8)
Potley Hill Primary School

I'VE BEEN IN THE SNOW

I've been in the snow
On a holiday I'll never forget
It had been snowing for ages
The snow had gone beyond my depth.

We had built a snowman
It was even taller than me
I had been out there for hours
And I was covered in snow from the tree.

Riding up the mountains
And skiing all the way down
I had a really big fall
And my skis went into the ground.

Up on the lifts, it was freezing
My hair had frozen stiff
Skiing down, really fast
I nearly went right off the cliff.

It will be a holiday to remember
Good and bad times in the snow
I'll keep a booklet of the holiday
To show my friends - just to show.

Jessica Stevens (10)
Potley Hill Primary School

MY CAT PURPLE

My cat Purple is a lazy old cat
She used to be thin but now she's fat
She's got a white line down her back
When you carry her she's like a sack
My cat Purple is a lazy old cat!

Louise Hesketh (8)
Potley Hill Primary School

A WHOLE NEW WORLD

Monday,
Wet, cold and miserable.
The back street walls painted in graffiti,
A vandalised car with peeling paint and broken windows
sits alone in a holly hedge,
Rusted cans and crumpled paper scattered
on the damp floor.
An ugly example of how we treat our world.

Tuesday,
The clouds have darkened over night, I woke up
to a new world,
The vandalised car coated in a thick layer of
gleaming white paint.
The vivid graffiti is framed by crystal icicles,
The rubbish transformed into mysterious sculptures.
Once more the world is a beautiful place.

Jonathan Moore (9)
Potley Hill Primary School

SAILOR'S LULLABY

The sailor's lullaby cries out
To rescue all
Takes the flames out of a fire
Takes the fun out of a cat and its mouse
Catches the anxiety of the salty air
Sets out to liberate tortured souls
Sings us to sleep.

Sophie Crisp (9)
Potley Hill Primary School

JOUSTING TOURNAMENT

I am a knight, a fearsome knight,
I ride my horse as fast as he goes,
I fought my way to the final,
I won some horses and trophies
I am a champion!

I have done some stunts to avoid lances,
Ducking and dodging,
I steer my horse with speed and agility.
Some men have died, some survived but fell from their horses.
I will enter the jousting competitions and hopefully get through.
I am the champion!

Alexander Allen (8)
Potley Hill Primary School

DOLPHINS

D eep
O cean
L arge
P lace
H arbour
I nlets
N orth
S ea.

Chelsea Rushton (8)
Potley Hill Primary School

THE GALE

Off went dustbin lids
As he howled
Like a cat
Around he prowled

Rubbish went flying
Down went trees
Roofs were shattered
Away went leaves

People were blown
Out of their beds
'I've done a lot of damage,'
The gale said.

'I am evil,
I am bad
I've made people
Very sad!'

Away went the gale
Away went he
Away he went
With a smile of glee.

Laura Hesketh (10)
Potley Hill Primary School

COMET THE HORNET

Comet travels at the speed that no man can see.
He has shields like armour plating that can stop a bullet in its tracks.
He's as shiny as a shooting star speeding across the sky,
And has eyesight like a hawk with binoculars.

Ross Peters (8)
Ropley CE Primary School

THE CHILDREN'S TREE

It's there in the forest,
They go there every day.
They called it the Children's Tree,
And it's still there today.

They went there after school one time,
To finally have some fun.
They found a little scarlet door
And in there were some buns.

They clambered through the door,
To see who might be there,
Instead of finding buns this time
They found a little chair.

Charlotte Mills (9)
Ropley CE Primary School

MY HAMSTER, MAISY

I have a hamster called Maisy,
She cannot be described as lazy.
She spins and spins and runs and runs
And eats her seed, like crazy.

I have a hamster called Maisy
She is as bright as a daisy,
In fact she is never hazy
And that's little Maisy.

Betty Glover (7)
Ropley CE Primary School

MY VERY BEST TREE

I love my favourite old beech tree in my garden,
It has a swing tied to one of its branches.
In summer I always play on my swing, for hours,
I sometimes hear the tree trying to talk to me.

I've always wanted to have a treehouse at the very top of it,
So I could see for miles and miles,
Next to it is a much smaller tree
And together, the tall trees make a little den
With their leaves

But I've always dreaded the time when it dies
Or gets chopped down!

Rosie Gisborne (7)
Ropley CE Primary School

MY BROTHER'S FERRET, FUZZ

Kieran's ferret is cream and grey
He goes a long, long way to play,
He has a friend whose name is Jill
But sometimes I'm afraid she's ill.

He kills rats and rabbits,
It's revolting when he does.
His friends call him Buzz
But his proper name is Fuzz!

Amie Webb (8)
Ropley CE Primary School

My Brilliant Butterfly Bird

As wobbly as a newborn foal trying to stand,
As elegant as a swan, swimming on a lake.
As light as a feather falling to the ground,
As tiny as the tiniest caterpillar's brain,
As amusing as a baby chimpanzee.
As fat as the fattest hippo, wallowing in mud,
As awkward as a bull in a china shop.

Jessica Hatch (8)
Ropley CE Primary School

Comet The Hornet

Comet the hornet is . . .
As fast as a cheetah with a jet pack,
As perceptive as a hawk with spy goggles,
As armoured as a tank with bullet deflectors,
And better camouflaged than an ant
With an invisibility cloak.
As dangerous as a hyena driving a tank
Into a nuclear power station.

Philip Bhol (9)
Ropley CE Primary School

The Palm Tree

On a beach near a desert there's a tree as free as a bee.
On the sea like a river, there's a boat going to float.
I climbed that tree and it seemed to say to me, 'Oi, get off me'.
I made a sandcastle out of sand, it was as big as a brass band.

Lucy Sutton (7)
Ropley CE Primary School

MY MARVELLOUS MASH

As slow as a tired tortoise
with superglue on all four feet.
As beautiful as a field of wild flowers,
As idle as a Labrador puppy,
lying by a warm fire.
As colourful as a clutter of butterflies
on a sunny day,
As smooth as a wet window
on a rainy day.
As warm as a roast dinner
which has just come out of an Aga.

Annabel Brooks (9)
Ropley CE Primary School

MY FLYING SCORPION

My flying scorpion is as dark as the night sky
when there is no moon,
As dangerous as a bomb, next to the fire,
As clever as nine brains but as dumb as a goldfish
with only one brain cell.
As powerful as Superman after he's been to the gym,
As fast as a dragster with no brakes or parachute.

Cameron Phillips (9)
Ropley CE Primary School

DELFA THE FLYING DELFIN

Delfa the flying Delfin is . . .
As cold as an iceberg with frostbite,
Like a speedboat racing in the sea with no brakes,
As smooth as cream that's been sieved,
As mean as coughs and colds.
As light as an imaginary feather,
As happy as a laughing hyena -
Who's been told the best joke in the world.
As small as an ant in a shrinking machine,
As fragile as a butterfly's wing in the stormy wind.

Natalie Culverwell (9)
Ropley CE Primary School

RIPLEY THE GREAT!

Ripley the colourful pig is . . .
As powerful as a robot with super strong arms,
As slow as a pig drowning in mud,
As small as a microscopic pin which has been cut in half,
As crazy as a chicken on a bad day,
As weird as a chimpanzee being chased by a banana,
As wicked as a DJ's Dad.
As colourful as the world's greatest rainbow,
As miserable as a baby who stayed up till ten o'clock,
As cheerful as birds which have learned a new song.

Georgie Davies (9)
Ropley CE Primary School

DELPHA THE FLYING DELFIN

Delpha the flying Delfin is . . .

As smooth as a newborn kitten,
She's faster than Concorde with ten jet-packs,
As much fun as a playful puppy with a shoe,
She's as magical as a unicorn in the most enchanted mist.
As friendly as a diving dolphin,
As light as a fluffy piece of cloud.
As sensible as a teacher's pet,
As elegant as a swan gliding on the lake,
She's as happy as a hyena who has been told
The funniest poem in the world.
She's as cute as a shy pony.

Abigail Nickless (9)
Ropley CE Primary School

DIGGER

Digger the dig . . .

Is as silent as a mouse in a mousehole,
As cuddly as a new white teddy.
As flexible as a fluffy dog, who has just had a bath.
As light as a feather in the sky,
As friendly as a young dolphin, playing
As ridiculous as a clown in a circus.

Zoe Hodgkinson (8)
Ropley CE Primary School

THE SUPERSONIC STAR

As amazing as Mr Goldie,
As fast as a cheetah with a jet-pack,
As colourful as a rainbow just made,
As dangerous as an electric power plant,
As tall as an elephant with crutches,
As brave as a rhino on waterskis,
As hungry as a rabbit with no food all day.

Jack Wyeth (10)
Ropley CE Primary School

SUPER SUNSET THE PINK CREATURE

Sunset is as fast as a 1000mph speeding bullet,
As mysterious as a tile falling off the roof at night,
As imaginative as a very intelligent brain,
As kind as a person with a frisky puppy,
As happy as an enormous hippo messing about in mud,
As loyal as a mother cat to her baby kittens,
As colourful as a sunset after a beautiful day.

Katie Adams (9)
Ropley CE Primary School

SUPER SUNSET, THE PINK CREATURE

Sunset is as fast as the fastest cheetah with eleven jet-packs on,
As intelligent as a guide dog in an obstacle course,
As kind as a best friend when you're stuck on a question,
As loyal as a gloop of supersonic glue that doesn't come off your skin,
As happy as a hyena that's just been told the world's funniest joke,
And as helpful as Mum when you're in peril.

Frances Smith (8)
Ropley CE Primary School

MY BICYCLE

My bicycle is a mountain bike
My bicycle is green
My bicycle is better than a car
My bicycle is clean

My bicycle is good at skidding
My bicycle is fast
But my bicycle got a puncture
And my bicycle came last

My bicycle is the best bicycle
My bicycle can fly
My bicycle has fourteen great gears
My bicycle flew high.

Guy Meager (8)
Ropley CE Primary School

POWERFUL PEGASUS

Pegasus the unicorn is . . .

As sleek as a hare on a diet,
As graceful as a swan gliding down the
moonlit lakes,
As beautiful as a sunset reflecting
on the river,
As mysterious as a door opening
for no reason.
As cold as the hills with snow sparkling on.

Beth Graham (9)
Ropley CE Primary School

POWERFUL PEGASUS

As stubborn as an ill mule,
As mysterious as Stonehenge at night.
As fast as grease lightning after eating mussels,
As hard as a stone, plated in steel.
He can be as slow as a weary tortoise on crutches.
As lonely as an old sock with its friend in the wash,
And as warm as the welcome given to all.

Jessica Hobbs (9)
Ropley CE Primary School

MY MIST MAKER

My mist maker is as blue as a summer sky,
Its tail is like a wiggly worm being stretched,
It's as intelligent as a packed dictionary,
Its fur is as silky as the finest silk,
As clumsy as a clown on ice skates,
As quiet as a hunting tiger.

Hannah Rodgers (9)
Ropley CE Primary School

WALTER THE FLYING DRAGON

He's as tall as Mount Everest on stilts.
He's as fussy as a baby with a bowl of sprouts.
He talks as much as a TV that can't be turned off.
He's as ugly as an ogre with make-up on.
He's as long-necked as a diplodocus.
He's as clever as Einstein on a good day.

Rhiannon Thomas (8)
Ropley CE Primary School

WHATIF?

(Based on 'Whatif' poem by Shel Silverstein)

Whatif the world was blue?
Whatif the sea was green?
Whatif the houses were completely flat?
Whatif the bullies weren't mean?

Whatif the teacher was nice to me?
Whatif she didn't nag?
Whatif she gave me sweets all day?
Whatif she gave me a bag?

Whatif the pandas were pink and green?
Whatif I hated you?
Whatif the grass was completely purple?
Whatif the sun was blue?

Whatif bread was green?
Whatif the sun was blue?
Whatif the world was completely flat?
Whatif milk was glue?

Whatif people were red?
Whatif cats were green?
Whatif dogs didn't bark at all?
Whatif I couldn't be seen?

Thea Arnott (7)
Ropley CE Primary School

THE WHOMPING WILLOW TREE

The whomping willow tree is twisty down to the steep ground.
I wonder if I will fall off the cliff of whomping willow tree.
Its enormous branches wave.
Maybe it's happy, maybe it's sad, or it's just having a bad time.
I climb this giant with lots of joy and as soon as I reach the top,
I jump to the ground.
Another willow tree, it says hello, it says goodbye, then whistles
in the wind.
Another willow tree, the twisty branches affect me.
The wind blows my hair. I look at the giant.
As I do that I think about it as a person.
The old hole is his mouth, the last two leaves his eyes and his nose
is an acorn hanging from a big branch.

Jessica Evans (7)
Ropley CE Primary School

MY BUTTERFLY BIRD

Dopey the butterfly bird . . .
Is as light as snow falling to Earth,
As colourful as a rainbow,
Sparkling in the sky after the rain.
As rapid as a racing car without a brake,
As courageous as a mouse trying
To get cheese from a mousetrap.
As solid as an elephant's tusk.

Abigail Joy Singleton (9)
Ropley CE Primary School

RIPLEY THE GREAT!

Ripley the colourful pig is . . .
. . . as speedy as a cheetah with a jet-pack,
. . . as tiny as a microscopic ant,
. . . as brainy as a teacher that's passed a very hard test,
. . . as light as an elephant in outer space,
. . . as wicked as a DJ's dad,
. . . as hungry as a lion who hasn't had a meal for a week.

Jessica Humm (8)
Ropley CE Primary School

BRONTO THE FLYING BULL

Bronto the flying bull is . . .
As strong as a muscular ox,
As sneaky as a hungry fox,
As kind as a newborn flower,
As tall as the Eiffel Tower,
As happy as a graceful butterfly,
As annoying as a buzzing fly,
As fast as racing cars.

Lizzie Flesher (8)
Ropley CE Primary School

WHATIF!
(Based on 'Whatif' by Shel Silverstein)

Whatif the world was made out of bread?
Whatif the world was red?
Whatif our teacher didn't talk at all?
We'd never know what he said.

William Cook (7)
Ropley CE Primary School

IF ONLY

If only I had what I wanted,
If only I were clever too,
If only I were bigger,
Then I would be just like you.

If only I had bigger meals,
If only I could grow,
If only I had more money,
That's what I'd like you to know.

If only I had tiny feet,
If only that was true,
That would be quite fantastic,
I might buy dainty shoes.

Claire Stratton (7)
Ropley CE Primary School

WHAT IF

What if I was lonely?
I want to play a game,
But I'm just too lonely,
So maybe you would play.

Then I might be happy,
I might find things to do,
There must be things much better,
Like playing games with you.

Kirsten Adams (7)
Ropley CE Primary School

LITTLE GIRL MOLLY

Molly loved sweets and her favourite was a lolly,
She had a dog and its name was Polly.
As she ate her sweets she felt very jolly,
She cuddled her dog as though it was a dolly.

Molly loved toys and her favourite was a car,
She had a bicycle and she rode it very far.
As she rode her bicycle she felt just like a star,
When she got hungry she would eat a chocolate bar.

Josh Wade (8)
Ropley CE Primary School

TELE THE SUPERSONIC TELEPORTER

Tele the supersonic teleporter is . . .
As kind as a sleeping flower on a sunny day.
As helpful as my kind mum who's just won the lottery.
As clever as a big-brained pig with five brains.
As jolly as a clown telling jokes.
As fast as the speed of light with a jet-pack on it.
As handsome as Henry VIII when he was young.
As brave as a knight fighting a dragon.

Simon Hunt (9)
Ropley CE Primary School

MY MIST MAKER

My mist maker is . . .
As velvety as a newborn kitten,
As intelligent as a scientist with an enormous brain,
As clumsy as a clown with a bucket of water on his head,
When he's in the water, he's as graceful as a dancing dolphin,
As white as a little cloud on a sunny day.

Catherine Gisborne (9)
Ropley CE Primary School

DIGORY THE MAN-EATING DOG

Digory the man-eating dog,
Is as dangerous as a mad bear driving a tank,
Is as fast as a cheetah with a jet-pack,
Is as tall as Mount Everest on stilts,
Is as soundless as James Bond with a silencer,
Is as active as an orang-utan who ate too much sugar,
Is as strong as a fit sumo wrestler.

George Harris (9)
Ropley CE Primary School

THE MAGNIFICENT ELIZABETH

As hot as a leopard sunbathing in Hawaii,
As energetic as a cheetah on a bike in the gym,
As slow as an armadillo with glue on its head, feet and toes,
As amusing as a monkey with a wig on,
As bad-tempered as an ape who lost a fight with a baby,
As loud as an elephant with a microphone.

Claire Bogan (8)
Ropley CE Primary School

WALTER THE FLYING DINOSAUR

Walter the flying dinosaur is . . .
Faster than Michael Schumacher on one of his best days,
Taller than the Empire State Building,
As unsteady as a baby learning to walk on stilts,
As loud as a howler monkey with a microphone,
Uglier than a troll with make-up on,
As fat as a hippo that's expecting twins,
As brainy as a calculator with extra batteries.

Faye Buckle (9)
Ropley CE Primary School

MAGNIFICENT MASH

Is as . . .
Slow as a tortoise with no legs!
Quiet as a mouse in church.
Sly as a fox, trying to keep his tail in a hunt.
Dreamy as a summer's day.
Light as a feather full of air.
Short as an ant who's been sat on by an elephant.
Careful as a spider weaving its web.

Elizabeth Pinniger (9)
Ropley CE Primary School

DRAGON

Amazing dragons
fly so very high from dawn till night
glittering, gliding, terrifying
through the dark night.

Max Tinkler (9)
St Peter's RC Primary School, Winchester

The Star

Shimmering star,
gleams like a light in a dark room.
Bright,
dazzling,
blazing.
A glittering angel dancing in the night's sky.

Philippa Falconer (9)
St Peter's RC Primary School, Winchester

The Moon

Sparkling moon
sparkles like a magnificent diamond
splendid
fantastic
wonderful.
A shining light in the night blue sky.

Jeneba Brewah (9)
St Peter's RC Primary School, Winchester

Golden Leaves

Golden leaves
falling off the autumn trees
when the crispy leaf touches the ground
where it meets its friends
safe and sound.

Ben Dexter (10)
St Peter's RC Primary School, Winchester

THE CAT

Home-owning cat
Pounces like a tiger about to get its
Prey
Sleek
Quick
Loved
Sound asleep.

Bethany Harrison (9)
St Peter's RC Primary School, Winchester

WET SHELL

Wet shell
glints like a turquoise sea in the dark.

Twinkling
sparkling
dazzling.

A beacon under the sea.

Shana Woodbridge (10)
St Peter's RC Primary School, Winchester

LUMINOUS STAR

Shining like a piece of glitter on a black page

Twinkling
Gleaming
Sparkling

A torch in the sky.

Charlotte Poffley (9)
St Peter's RC Primary School, Winchester

A STAR

A bright star
Twinkling like a brilliant crystal

Sparkling
Shining
Gleaming

A beautiful light in the dark sky.

Emily Rogers (10)
St Peter's RC Primary School, Winchester

OCEAN

Calming ocean
As peaceful as the night sky
Incredible
Breathtaking
Outstanding
A vast oasis away from
The crowd and the city.

Nicholas Sommer
St Peter's RC Primary School, Winchester

LIGHT

Abrupt light
Swift as an eagle upon a high mountain wind
Rapid
Rash
Hasty
A bright beacon that shatters the gathering gloom.

Danny Foy (9)
St Peter's RC Primary School, Winchester

TREES

Magnificent trees like beautiful giants keeping calm and still

Welcoming
Colourful
Pretty

Urban leaves and gorgeous blossoms.

Toby Coen (10)
St Peter's RC Primary School, Winchester

THE RAIN

Powerful rain
Forces like an eagle gliding down to land
Strength
Speed
Might
Strong water dripping from the sink.

Monique Martin (9)
St Peter's RC Primary School, Winchester

SHARP TEETH

Sharp teeth
like razor-sharp blades of steel
luminous
glowing
glittering
a jagged mountain in the snow.

Nicholas Kidd (10)
St Peter's RC Primary School, Winchester

THE STAR

Glittering star,
shines like a flash of lightning
beaming
sparkling
glowing
like a candle caught in the wind
a torch flying through the air.

Jordan Dempsey (10)
St Peter's RC Primary School, Winchester

RADIANT MOON

Radiant moon,
shine like a blazing sun.
Luminous.
Beam.
Glow.

A gigantic white ball on a big, dark, shadowy sky.

Luke Duff (9)
St Peter's RC Primary School, Winchester

SCALY FISH

Scales like a multicoloured rainbow
Shining
Shimmering
Glistening
Swimming as fast as a shark in attack.

Bethan Steane (10)
St Peter's RC Primary School, Winchester

FIRE

Wood dweller
Heat bringer
Water dier
Coal user
Chimney smoker
Burn creator
Cold stealer
Paper killer.

Erika Hoffman (10)
St Peter's RC Primary School, Winchester

CUPID

Match maker,
Hopeful lover,
Love finder,
Romance helper,
Heartache breaker,
Arrow shooter,
Heart softener,
Son of Venus.

Claire Mills (10)
St Peter's RC Primary School, Winchester

LOVE

A loving sweetheart
A Valentine creator
A friend former
A heart hunter.

Lydia Ricketts (10)
St Peter's RC Primary School, Winchester

THE MOON

The moon
Comforting face
Like God looking from Heaven
Makes you feel safe
Like an everlasting beacon
A proud face
Looking upon its world
Lighting it up like hope
An army of crystals glittering behind it
A great eye
A dreamy eye
A beacon of hope.

George Tutton (11)
St Peter's RC Primary School, Winchester

HAMSTER

Furry beast,
Nut cracker,
Food chomper,
Hand juggler,
Athletic animal,
Wheel runner,
That's me.

Danielle Stainer (11)
St Peter's RC Primary School, Winchester

GOD

God Almighty
He died to save our sins
Almighty, always there, never-ending love
Always there like a part of our body
Always there like my best friend
It makes me feel lucky to be alive
Like a light always shining upon me
God Almighty
Reminds us how important our life is.

Emma Buckett (9)
St Peter's RC Primary School, Winchester

DOLPHIN

Shaped fin,
blue leather,
swift swimmer,
water lover,
loving creature,
leading mother,
acrobatic diver,
playful splasher.

Almariza Menton (10)
St Peter's RC Primary School, Winchester

LION RAGE

The great lion.
Magnificent king of the jungle.
Strong, powerful, almighty.
A tyrant bringing down an endless reign of terror.
As swift as the wind, as powerful as a raging forest fire.
Makes me feel as limp and weak as an ant in the long grass.
The great lion.
Making all of civilisation look as ordinary as a splinter
                                        in a wooden door.

David McHardy (10)
St Peter's RC Primary School, Winchester

PANTHER

Black beast
Savage slayer
Lay in ambush
Tree climber
Bird slasher
Flesh ripper
Silent creeper
Jungle prowler.

James Mahood (11)
St Peter's RC Primary School, Winchester

LOVE

Something special
Something sweet
Something romantic
Something to care for
Something to treasure
Something to be fond of
Something which will never fade
Something very affectionate
Something meaningful
Something pure.

Lynne Moreto (11)
St Peter's RC Primary School, Winchester

WIND

A leaf blower
A rain caster
A destruction bringer
A window rattler
A kite flyer
A paper Hoover
A tree rustler
A flag waver
A branch breaker.

Luke Kingshott-Taylor (10)
St Peter's RC Primary School, Winchester

MONKEY

Tree swinger
Leaf rustler
Grass racer
Bush hider
Food scavenger
Fruity eater
Tail swayer
Animal tormentor
Innocent creature.

Francesca Wild (11)
St Peter's RC Primary School, Winchester

DOLPHIN

A smooth glider
a sea prancer
a dream leaper
a synchronised swimmer
a disabled treasure
a human carer
an acrobatic lover
a jumping supreme.

Kate Eastham (10)
St Peter's RC Primary School, Winchester

THE SUN

Leaf wilter
Ice melter
Heat bringer
Light giver
Dark killer
Rain evaporator
Plant murderer
An object of interest.

James Fenton (10)
St Peter's RC Primary School, Winchester

CAT

Black cat
purring like a lion roaring
playful
furry
scratchy
sleeping all day.

Bethany Rose (9)
St Peter's RC Primary School, Winchester

CANDLE

Smoky candle
burns like a lonely star in the night
flashing
gleaming
silent
a torch that lights the way.

Lauren Sanders (9)
St Peter's RC Primary School, Winchester

THE OWL OF THE NIGHT

Gliding through the fog of the forest,
The owl approaches his prey.
With his menacing eyes gazing,
Swoops swiftly with the wind on his wings, talons open ready to swipe.
A scavenger perching in a high and mighty tree.
Wings huddled to his chest,
Beak, razor-sharp and deadly,
Looking down onto the dull and deserted earth.
When morning comes the owl flees to his warm and welcoming nest,
Where he will sleep until night comes once more.

Elise West (10)
St Peter's RC Primary School, Winchester

FRIENDS

They help you if you're feeling down
They are always there to help you
They keep you going
Friendship maker!
They make you laugh
They entertain you
You can trust them
They stick up for you
What am I thinking of?
You!

James Kearney (10)
St Peter's RC Primary School, Winchester

LIGHTNING

Lightning, bolt of lightning,
Piercing through the clouds like a cat's claw,
Dagger-like, razor-sharp,
Deadly but beautiful,
A threatening carving knife in the ink-black sky.

Sitting in the clouds, deciding its victim,
It dashes for the life below,
A flash, a shock,
Making your heart jump,
It rapidly soars in the air.

Evil and sharp,
Like teeth digging into your skin,
It pinches you,
Giving you a chill,
Blood rushes to your neck,
A shiver down your spine,
Making you shudder.

It clashes with the calm, clear, night sky,
Spontaneous, hasty, headlong,
Like a jet at full speed,
Expeditious and determined,
A hawk over its prey.

Slowly floating away,
To somewhere, we do not know.
For it could bring terror,
Or just hover overhead,
Drained and weary,
It drifts into the horizon,
Lightning, bolt of lightning.

Mary Barlow (10)
St Peter's RC Primary School, Winchester

A SECRET

A secret is a thing,
That always knows,
A thing,
That always keeps.
A thing,
To be kept safe,
To be cherished.
Too special to be held,
Like a sparkling jewel,
Filling your mind
With a special feeling
Of joy,
Of warmth,
A soft touch, gently stroking,
Calming,
Soothing,
Never to be told.

Katy Palmer (11)
St Peter's RC Primary School, Winchester

WHITE HORSES OF THE MOON

The white horses of the moon lash through the waves.
Pounding their hooves against the icy surface of the sea.
Go now, white beasts, fly through the waves.
Strain your greatest
And smash the perfect mirror of the ocean.

Valerija Custance (11)
St Peter's RC Primary School, Winchester

THE GREAT LION

Lion
Golden, fierce, mighty,
Like a mountain over the world,
Like the sun over all the stars,
It makes me feel small and insignificant,
Like a child all alone in a crowd,
Lion,
King of all animals.

Zoë Morgan (10)
St Peter's RC Primary School, Winchester

LOVE FOR VALENTINE'S DAY

A heart pounder
A love attracter
A heart hunter
A good admirer
A person's wooer
A loving sweetheart
A life companion
A romance maker.

Karim Kazane (11)
St Peter's RC Primary School, Winchester

LOVE

Something special
Something meaningful
Something affectionate
Which is personal
Something sweet
Something needed
Something cute
Which you cherish.

Rosie Clayden (10)
St Peter's RC Primary School, Winchester

FRIENDS

Helping hand
Caring for you
Loving helper
Fun player
Sticking up for you
Helping you when you fall
Being there when you need them
And having each other.

May Sawyer (9)
St Peter's RC Primary School, Winchester

SNAKE'S FEATURES

Smoothly slithering on the hot desert sand
Quick
Deadly
Poisonous
Scales like an overlapping mosaic

Fangs
Long and sharp like a skin-piercing dagger
Menacing
Blood-dripping
Droplets
Like a black drop of ink on a snow-white page

Scales
A rainbow of colours
Green
Red
Purple
Colours clashing like cymbals crashing
A snake, not a creature to mess with.

Lizzie Underwood (11)
St Peter's RC Primary School, Winchester

GRANDFATHER CLOCK

Old clock
ticks like a falling drop of water when it hits the ground
ticking
tocking
donging
an old church bell.

David McKenna (9)
St Peter's RC Primary School, Winchester

THE SWAN

The swan,
She is waiting for him,
But will he ever come?
She is full of hope,
She has waited for days,
She does not know,
She will wait forever,
Yet he will not come,
She is still faithful,
She is waiting for him,
The swan.

Isabel Ronaldson (10)
St Peter's RC Primary School, Winchester

WAR

Men fighting. Men dead.
Boys fighting. Boys dead.
People running from the explosion of bombs.
People dying like ants.

Fighting,
Panic,
Fear,

Why do we have war?

Jack McCabe (9)
St Peter's RC Primary School, Winchester

BABIES

Cool crawler,
Super scribbler,
Creative crier,
Unsilent sleeper,
Waddling walker,
Maniac muncher,
Unclean creeper,
Superb slumberer,
Enormous eater,
Mess maker,
Lullaby lover.

Caitlin O'Kelly (9)
St Peter's RC Primary School, Winchester

MY DEN

A dull, dark place to hide away,
A secret room to go and play.

A den so deep, down under ground,
I could hide for months and never be found.

A place to shelter when it rains,
And get away from all life's pains.

A den to go and be alone,
But know you're not too far from home.

That's what I built my den for!

Stephanie High (10)
St Peter's RC Primary School, Winchester

THE MOON

Moon
Street lighter
A path guider
Bright
Beautiful
Radiant
Like an almighty torch hovering above the Earth
Like a white spill on black paper
I'm peaceful
Staring out into the night
I feel as small as an ant against the bleak and starry sky
Moon
It reminds me of just how wonderful our world is!

Lily Stead (9)
St Peter's RC Primary School, Winchester

BLACK PANTHER

A mysterious murderer
Like silk to your fingertips
Lithe
Ferocious
Ruthless
The colour of ebony
Waiting to pursue his next victim
Death inevitable.

Jade Coward (10)
St Peter's RC Primary School, Winchester

SINISTER DEATH

Sinister death
Waiting to wreck another family's future
Like a sword hanging above someone's head, waiting to drop
The dark lord that nobody can refute
Unguarded, no way to stop him doing his job
Fearless
Brings a dark cloud over his next victim
Then in a split second his victim is gone . . .
Eaten up by a careless carnivore
No value, just a spirit in the wind.

Joe Lewis (11)
St Peter's RC Primary School, Winchester

FEARSOME SHARK

Nature's colossal eating machine
Bloodcurdling
Chilling
Destructive
The swift sea monster from the deep
Ferocious
Carnivorous
Evaporating and then coming out at you when you're not looking
Conqueror of the ocean, none can oppose it.

Duncan Bray (11)
St Peter's RC Primary School, Winchester

NIGHT

Dreamy night,
The moon drapes the Earth with silken light,
The nightingale's song cuts through the misty air,
The stars' beauty twinkles soft and rare,
Peace, harmony and tranquillity.

Black storm clouds
As dark as a thief's heart,
Stealing silver light from the moon,
Robbing the stars one by one,
Heavy, damp, oppressive.
The sun glows red as dawn chases away the night.

Alex Gambrill (10)
St Peter's RC Primary School, Winchester

PANTHER

Breath thief
Deliberate bully
Meat tearer
Innocent destroyer
First-rate carnivor
Heart pounder
Jet-black stalker
Non-stop murderer.

Aicha Zaa (11)
St Peter's RC Primary School, Winchester

HALLOWE'EN

Stuck.
Stuck.
Stuck on a hill,
All alone,
I can see shadows moving around me.
I close my eyes, hoping for it to be a nightmare.
Nothing happens.
I open them, I'm still there.
I feel a cold breath on my shoulders,
An icy wind.
Pretending nothing's there, I close my eyes,
Hoping for it to be a nightmare.
Nothing happens.
I see bats flitting in the moonlight.
I hear a long, chilling screech.
It's only an owl, I tell myself,
I close my eyes, hoping for it to be a nightmare.
Nothing happens.
I'm stuck here.
Stuck.
Stuck.
Stuck on a hill on
Hallowe'en!

Katherine Nahajski (10)
St Peter's RC Primary School, Winchester

CREATING MANKIND

Creator of life coming to Earth
Coming down to seek new birth
What we're made up of, what we are
Swirling in a shooting star

Maker of life, it first began
And now it's ended up as man
Particles, molecules, tiny bits
Land on Earth when the meteor hits

Look at someone, look at their face
Then look at the rocks from outer space
In the future as in the past
The next meteor you see could be your last!

James Thorpe (11)
St Peter's RC Primary School, Winchester

HOPE

Helping us, guiding us, a beacon of light,
Showing us the way to better things.
When life is dark, hope is bright,
Giving us use of our wings.

Hope is telling us to never give up,
Telling us to keep on going,
Hope is telling us never to stop,
For hope is always glowing.

Barbara Speed (11)
St Peter's RC Primary School, Winchester

THE MAGPIE

A tree waver,
A grass hopper,
A shiny scraper,
Dark,
Mysterious,
Haunted,
Great,
As it sings its song,
A sorrow seeker,
A joy maker,
It makes a girl glaze
And a boy bash,
A silver snatcher,
A gold stealer,
A secret saver,
A kisser of kings,
A winning wisher,
A feather friend,
A wise special bird that should never end.

Rosie Fagan (10)
St Peter's RC Primary School, Winchester

MY SECRET

I have a secret
And I'm not going to tell
I shall keep my voice
Locked up as a cage
I will only write it down
On a secretive page
I have a secret
And I'm not going to tell.

Hillie Nouwens (9)
St Peter's RC Primary School, Winchester

A HORROR MOVIE

Chills are running up my spine,
The music's melting into my ears,
Making me want to scream . . .

Nothing happens.
Names start running down the blank screen . . .

I might choose a romance next time.

Claire Whitfield (10)
St Peter's RC Primary School, Winchester

THE LIGHT

The light
A magical barrier of midnight rays
Bright
Unbreakable
Unbearable
A dazzling substance of Heaven and Earth.

Mary Sims-Howlett (10)
St Peter's RC Primary School, Winchester

THE MIGHTY MOUNTAIN

The mighty mountain,
As tall as a giant,
As ferocious as a lion,
Gigantic, monstrous, unthinkable,
Makes you think it's going to collapse,
Makes you think, *does it ever stop going up?*
Makes you feel like a speck in the horizon.

Amelia Thomson (10)
St Peter's RC Primary School, Winchester

THE CITY THAT NEVER SLEEPS

Twinkling lights,
Like stars in the night sky.
Shining,
Flashing,
Beaming,
Dazzling,
A wonder to our eyes.

The night's alive,
Like a club in the city.
Laughter,
Shouting,
Crying,
Traffic,
In a city that never sleeps.

Georgina Falconer (11)
St Peter's RC Primary School, Winchester

THE GLOWING MOON

The glowing moon
High in the sky
Lonely, mournful, eerie,
Like a white spill on a black page
Like a silver plate high in the sky
It makes me feel watched over
Like someone really cares
The glowing moon
Makes me think how lucky we are.

Ellen Culhane (11)
St Peter's RC Primary School, Winchester

TEDDY BEAR

Teddy bear
Always there for a cuddle
Like music to your heart
Warm, soft, knowing
Like a little ray of sunshine
Amongst the fear and worry
In the centre of your heart
An essential part of your life
Ready for you to spill your heart out.

Isla Dixon (10)
St Peter's RC Primary School, Winchester

PANDAS

Pandas, they're cute and fluffy, they love to eat bamboo
Pandas can swim although you wouldn't think so and
They're also very shy.
I love pandas, they're so sweet, they live in China and love to eat.

I love pandas, they're so *neat!*

Jake Kelly & Shannon Wootton (9)
Somerton Middle School

THE BOY IN MY CLASS

There once was a boy in my class,
His teeth were made out of glass,
He chewed on a kid
And a dustbin lid,
But his favourite meal was grass.

Katie Williamson & Sophie Bull (9)
Somerton Middle School

THERE ONCE WAS AN OLD MAN FROM MARS

There once was an old man from Mars
Who was made of chocolate bars.
He was walking along the street,
He wanted to buy some sweets,
But he didn't have any money,
So he stole some honey,
But he dropped it on the floor,
So he had to steal some more
Chocolate bars.

Lucy Morris & Sarah Tuckwell (9)
Somerton Middle School

THE OLD MAN FROM MARS

There was an old man from Mars,
Who said he could eat lots of cars.
But when he bit in,
He made such a din,
The silly old man from Mars.

Megan Crews & Jordan Ayton (9)
Somerton Middle School

THE MAN FROM MARS

There once was a man from Mars
Who loved to eat chocolate bars
He bit on a block
Whilst wearing a frock
Then reached up to bite on the stars.

Chelsea Harrison (9)
Somerton Middle School

BING BANG BAILEY

Bing Bang Bailey shook his head,
Then decided he was dead.
When he found that he was wrong,
He ran away and then was gone.

Next day when he went into town,
Everyone else was in their gown,
But when he went into a shop,
The shopkeeper said, 'Hip, hap, hop.'

Bing Bang Bailey shook his head,
Then decided he was dead.
When he found that he was wrong,
He ran away and then was gone.

So then I asked him, 'What's your name?'
'I don't know, I'm insane.'
He then proceeded down the street,
And tripped and fell over his own feet.

Bing Bang Bailey shook his head,
Then decided he was dead.
When he found that he was wrong,
He ran away and then was gone.

Elizabeth Kelly & Emily Dale (10)
Somerton Middle School

MAN IN THE TREE

There once was a man in a tree house
His singing scared off his own mouse
He ate seaweed
Had his mouse on a lead
The mouse had his own little house.

Molly Burnip (9)
Somerton Middle School

THERE ONCE WAS A MAN FROM THE MOON

There once was a man from the moon
Who had a big pet baboon
He had no hair and
His body was bare
And now he's named after the moon
And now he's named after the moon.

Kathryn Bunker (9) & Annabel Randall (10)
Somerton Middle School

THE SOUNDS IN MY HOUSE

Inside my house
The stairs are creaking
And
The kettle is bubbling.
My sister is moaning.
My bed is banging.
The floor is blazing
And
The house is full of noises.
The noises are scary.
The fire is zapping hard
And
My dad is snoring.
It's so terrible, he makes the whole house shake.
I have bats in the attic,
They squeak like a mouse,
So I hide under my covers all night!

Alexandra Moore (8)
The Grey House School

DAYTIME NOISE

In the daytime,
In the autumn.
Sounds I can hear,
Rustling in the bushes,
Sniffing in the big, round apple tree.
In the old autumn wood
Bumblebees are buzzing
And
Laughing from some children hitting at a
Big, round apple tree.
For in the old wood,
Rustling, buzzing and laughing
You can hear for miles.

Louise Ingham (8)
The Grey House School

QUIET SOUNDS

Birds are singing
Squirrels are nibbling
Hedgehogs rustling in the bushes
Quiet sounds are peaceful sounds
Baby birds are cracking out of their eggs
Then rain starts to fall, pitter-pattering softly on the ground
Then in the humming sunshine the birds begin to sing
Then all begins again.

Cameron Gaul (7)
The Grey House School

THE SOUNDS I HEAR IN MY HOUSE

B aby Fiona sucking her milk bottle.
A fter our tea my brother, Matt, frantically tries to complete
                                              a level on a game.
B aby Fiona cries if she does not get her own way.
Y ou shouldn't wake Fiona from her sleep.

F inally she is asleep and we can rest.
I love baby Fiona as much as I love my whole family.
O ften she cries a lot, but not today.
N o noise when she's asleep.
A fter all that we can rest and go to sleep.
   Zzzzzzzzzzzz.

Alex Bruce (8)
The Grey House School

THE SEA

The sea is calm and cool against my feet,
running water trickling over
in the cool summer's breeze
like a velvet cover over my feet, so delicate,
almost like rose petals, so soft.
Then a storm breaks out
and a mighty storm it is,
devouring every ship in sight,
tall or small, green or brown.
The waves are as tall as skyscrapers
reaching out to the sky like a bird,
soaring higher and higher,
then crashing down through lack of support
and building up to try again
but still falling down.

Philippa Gleadow (10)
The Grey House School

THE EARTH

The Earth is like a beautiful green apple floating around an
                                        orange fireball.
The grass swishes with the wind like seaweed (swishing) in the sea.
The sky is blue like shimmering pearls.
The sea is like millions of horses galloping towards you, then
                turning into writhes of water in between your feet.
The trees are like giants swaying to and fro.
The leaves are all sorts of beautiful colours: gold, orange, brown
                            and green, all floating to the ground.
The snow is like a white sheet covering everything.
The clouds are like fluffy toys.
Sand is like little grains of gold.
Stars are little lights in the night sky, twinkling in the silent night.
Rain pours down like wet stones, leaving behind a beautiful rainbow
                of red, orange, green, blue, indigo and violet.
As the sun comes out again and the children come out to play.

Jemima Ridley (10)
The Grey House School

PLAYGROUND NOISES

In the playground
Children are yelling,
Teachers are shouting,
The wind is humming,
(At my house, Dad is snoring.)
The rain is pouring.
It really is annoying
When the whistle goes.
Playtime is over!

Andrew Rankin (8)
The Grey House School

THE SOUNDS IN MY BEDROOM

The creaking of my bed gives me the creeps.
Just as I get into bed the noise starts.
The buzzing of the telephone.
The blasting of the TV.
I can never get to sleep.
Honestly.
But when that all stops,
I hear the stomping of my parents coming up to bed.
Then it is the worst part - the snoring of my dad.
It booms through the whole house.
I am surprised my mum can get to sleep.
But now she's taken my side and given me a pair of ear muffs.
That's good.

Alice Rudland (7)
The Grey House School

JUNGLE SOUNDS

Bushbabies wailing
Monkeys chattering
Cheetahs thundering
Lions roaring
Leopards lurking
Rhinos raging
Zebras drinking
But worst of all
Sssssss . . .

Jonathan Manson (8)
The Grey House School

A WINTER'S MORNING

Winter is cold and crisp
With layers of snow which have
Fallen onto branches of trees
And icicles hanging from fences and gates.

Winter feels like there has been a huge
White blanket thrown over the earth.
Robins, cold, hopping along the path
With their feathers all fluffed up to keep warm.

Winter is beautiful
When the sun shines brightly on the trees.
And slowly, very slowly,
The snow starts to melt.

Winter is fading and
The snowmen start to melt.
The snow on the trees start melting
More and more until -
Spring is here!

Georgia Pike (11)
The Grey House School

SNOWFLAKE

Look at me!
    I'm a pretty little snowflake,
Falling from the sky.
    I don't want to melt
But look at me, look at me.
    I'm a pretty little snowflake so
        Look at me!

Emily Fearon (9)
The Grey House School

SNOW POEM

Snow is calm and peaceful.
Trees are bare, tall and grey.
Snow is pretty and white.
Winter is cold.
Snow is quiet and wet.
Snow is soft and tasty, clean and misty.
Snow is fun to play in,
Chilly for a walk,
Snow drifts from the sky,
And falls to the floor.
Snow is when you wear hat,
Gloves and a coat.
Snow is pretty.

Tara Kirby (8)
The Grey House School

SNOW

The snow this morning
Got quite boring
But now it's bigger, better.
It's bigger!
The icicles are on the edge of our door,
The snow is piling in.
My dad had to get his spade.
I hope it snows tomorrow.
It's freezing!

William Long (8)
The Grey House School

A Winter Morning

One day I wake up and see a blanket covering our lawn.
A robin on a low branch chirping an icy winter tune.
Animals very well hidden from view, yet they can see you.
Staring out into the garden on this spectacular morning.

The snow is falling, falling, falling, the white snow queen has come.
Abandoned nests will not be used on this chilly morning.
No birds will come out to play, except the robin, bold yet very small.
Staring out into the garden on this spectacular morning.

There is no school today, no maths lessons, they're a long way away.
Flights are delayed, even the ones in the other countries.
I rush outside to play in the blanket covering our lush green lawn.
Staring out into the garden on this spectacular day.

The snow, not knowing it is slowly dying, melting away slowly.
People standing there watching the snow shrivelling up.
The sun comes out from behind a cloud and finishes off the snow.
Staring out into the garden on that spectacular morning.

Tom Coussins (10)
The Grey House School

Why I Like Winter

I like winter because it is nearly Christmas
I like to see the children playing in the snow.
I like making snow angels and throwing
Snowballs at my sister
And putting snow down her back.
I like having hot chocolate, the warmth of the drink.
Watching the good movies on TV
And having fun in the snow,
Looking forward to Christmas.

Chloe Young (9)
The Grey House School

THE MYSTIC FOREST

In the mystic forest lies an evil snake,
an ant will crawl up your hand and suck your blood,
vines will grab you and pull you down,
the next thing you know you're in a big spider's web.

In the mystic forest you will be eaten up,
giant spiders come after you,
in the forest lie bones and skulls which
come alive and start to attack you.

In the forest, trees come alive
and make scary noises
suddenly you're in a pit and can't come out
leaves wrap you up and you can't get free.

In the mystic forest, zombies roam about,
and you see eyes looking at you,
and if you ever go in the mystic forest
beware!

Krishan Pujara (10)
The Grey House School

SNOWBOARDING

When it is cold
Snow falls down.
I go outside and turn
My skateboard upside down.
I take the wheels off,
Turn it up the right way,
I'm ready to go outside
To have lots of fun.

Ben Cutler (8)
The Grey House School

IF I HAD TO PICK A VALENTINE

If I had to pick a valentine
someone from afar,
I don't think you know
but you're my shining star.

If I had to pick a valentine
someone who is true,
I hope you know that
I would always choose you.

If I had to pick a valentine
someone who would stand by me,
I hope you would be
the one I could see.

If you had to pick a valentine
and you didn't know who,
I just want you to know
I would always choose you.

If you had to pick a valentine
and your friends would ask,
'Who is she?' I hope you
would say me.

If you had to pick a valentine
Who would it be?
I hope you would
definitely choose me.

Isobel Frodsham (10)
The Grey House School

SWEETY LAND

The king of spades sailed on the sea,
In a beautiful turtle-shaped boat.
Suddenly a shark jumped out of the sea,
And jumped to steal his coat!

In the bong-tree forest,
The king saw a baby with a weird belly.
The king jumped with joy and ate it at once,
For it was made out of jelly!

The king saw the gingerbread village,
The huts were made out of toffee.
The king went inside and had a small bite,
And thought that it tasted like coffee!

The king took a ride on a chocolate bunny,
That hopped about like a spring.
A villager passed by on a horse made of sweets,
The villager looked at the king and said, 'Ping!'

It was finally time for the king to go,
He rode on a dolphin across the sea.
When the king got home, he suddenly thought
He wouldn't have space for tea!

Daniel Funnell (10)
The Grey House School

THE STORM

The storm was raging and shouting out loud.
'I am the king of all kings,' he said,
'I will defeat everyone in my way and destroy them.'
Everyone ran and ducked away.
The sun stayed in bed all day, but when he heard
He ran to find the storm.
The sun and the storm were fighting,
Sun and rain were coming from the sky,
The storm was like a massive monster covering the world
But with small hints of sunshine everywhere.
At last though the storm got tired and gave in,
Vanishing but leaving behind a beautiful rainbow.
The sun shone prouder than ever and did so for the rest of the week.

Ilana de Jouvencel (10)
The Grey House School

MIDNIGHT OWL

I hear her screeching whistle
Like the midnight owl
As the bluebells close their petals to sleep.
I can hear the last of the squirrel trying to crack her nuts,
And the sun turns into the moon.
As the sky turns dark blue-sapphire,
The midnight is here with its midnight owl.

Katharine Whittingham (7)
The Grey House School

THE BATTLE OF ZEUS

The sand is dry and the sun shines down,
Two tense armies waiting for the battle to begin.
Suddenly the battle horn sounds,
Man vs Myth, who will win?

Minotaurs, cyclops and centaurs roar,
Men grip swords and plunge in.
Weapons plunge into flesh,
Man vs Myth, who will win?

Cyclops grab men and throws them miles,
Minotaurs' horns pierce soldiers' skin.
Centaurs rain arrows onto men,
Man vs Myth, who will win?

Spears are thrown through cyclops' heads,
Swords of man plunge in.
Dead bodies lie on the blood-drenched ground,
Man vs Myth, who will win?

Thomas Kelly (11)
The Grey House School

LUNCH NOISES

Munching, nibbling goes the food
And
Crunching, sizzling in the kitchen.
Dribbling from the tap,
Banging from saucepans.
Now the bell rings
Shouting and yelling is heard.

George Bertuzzi-Glover (8)
The Grey House School

THERE'S A CASTLE ON THE HILLTOP

There's a castle on the hilltop,
With ghouls and ghosts inside,
Also there are skeletons to scare you . . .
From behind!

There's a castle on the hilltop,
Nobody dares go in,
But if you're brave and risk your life,
Just stroll on right in.

There's a castle on the hilltop,
And I've just walked right in,
Oh I wish, I wish I hadn't,
Though the only way out is in.

There's a castle on the hilltop,
I'm now trapped inside,
I am so stupid for doing this,
I know I'll be eaten *alive!*

There's a castle on the hilltop,
I'm walking up the stairs,
Past suits of armour, doors, one window,
I think I'll soon expire,
(From all this lack of sun).

Michael Parsons (10)
The Grey House School

MOLLY MOUNTAIN

On Molly Mountain everything goes wrong,
The animals have changed!

The main predator is Rocky Rabbit
Who has fangs the size of his legs!
He can kill a wolf with one swipe of his paw
And scares humans on his travels.

Willing Wolf is a kind, patient vegetarian
Who would do anything for shrubs to eat,
Moves fast when it's getting cold
And runs from rabbits a lot.

Cunning Caribou is a quick and sly creature
Who lives in packs of about ten.
They love eating bears
And often, if hungry, eat humans!

Boring Bear is a dull type of animal
Who hops around eating carrots,
Weeps when humans run
And misses his home in a hutch.

Molly Mountain is terrible for humans,
They always go to stroke rabbits
Who just bite off their heads!
The rabbits when in captivity (if caught) can be a handful!
They break the hutches open and destroy the whole house!
It's a complete disaster -
But then the witches come back.
They completely change the mountain back,
Every single animal!
And then with a swish of their brooms
They turn back with pots full of gold!

Craig Judd (10)
The Grey House School

A WINTER'S DAY

One winter day it snowed,
Snow all over the country,
In Wales and Scotland, everywhere;
The snow fell and fell,
Some schools were closed,
Some children turned up late,
Because they were snowed in.

Havoc on the roads, accidents,
Crashes, trains stopped, flights cancelled,
Buses late - the ones that run,
Abominable traffic, one lane open
At some motorways, and some closed.

Freezing, frozen, fields of farms,
Icicles hanging from roofs;
Squirrels at the bottom of trees
Come out from hibernation;
Ducks waddle on frozen ponds,
My dog walking on it too,
Cracking it, and the ducks don't;
Children building snowmen,
Having snowball fights.

Soaking wet is everybody,
They go in and put warmer clothes on,
Gloves and hats are essential and jackets,
A winter's day that's today,
A winter's day that's enough for today.

Henry Appleton (10)
The Grey House School

MY FIRST DAY AT SCHOOL

My first day at school was absolutely terrible,
I woke up feeling slightly on edge,
but when I got there, assembly had already begun,
so it wasn't a good start.
The headmaster called me to his office,
and asked rather severely why I was late.
I said, 'I forgot to brush my teeth.'
He just didn't care what the excuse was.

Later I got into a fight with a boy
(in the classroom)
so the teacher said, 'Go to the headmaster now!'
So now I was in for it.
I went back to that same place again and knocked.
'Come in,' said a voice.
I walked in and saw the headmaster reading a book.
'So we meet again,' said the same droning voice.
'I got into a fight with a boy,' I said.
So that was it.
The headmaster called my mum and I went home at only 11 o'clock.
And that was a record!

Tommy Wilson (11)
The Grey House School

THE OAK TREE

I am as strong as a lion prowling through the bush,
As big as a house standing proud,
My leaves are as green as grass on a summer's day,
My bark is as brown as a bear fishing for salmon,
I whistle in the wind,
I am as old as the world itself,
I used to be an acorn lying on the ground,
I was used as wood for the big boats in the old days,
If ever they knew me they would never have cut me down,
I never lie on the ground, not even to die,
In a forest I am the one who stands out,
I am an oak tree.

Matthew Fisher (11)
The Grey House School

ALLITERATION

One wiggly worm wiggling like mad,
Two thick trees having their bark taken,
Three thin tramps walking on the street,
Four flinging ferrets flying above the flowers,
Five fattish farmers falling off a cliff,
Six silly sausages in a steaming pan,
Seven smelly seagulls diving into the sea,
Eight enormous eggs having egg bread,
Nine naughty Nik-Naks crisps are noisily noshed
Ten trembling tanks blowing up the talking toilets.

Adam Perryman (10)
The Grey House School

THE MEANING OF CHRISTMAS

Christmas means happiness, presents and joy
For every child, girl and boy.
Chocolate log and Christmas food,
Then sweets and sausages are chewed,
Tree with holly all around
And mistletoe all in a mound.

Santa from the chimney deep
Leaves a spell so all won't weep.
Food and presents cram his sack,
Chest of presents behind his back.

Yet without Jesus, God or love
All this would not be,
For God's love is like a dove
But never flies away.

Guy Bishop (9)
The Grey House School

ALLITERATION

One weak worm whistled weakly.
Two tired twins transferred a tarantula.
Three teenagers turned on the television.
Four fairies flew to Finland.
Five forks fell onto a falcon's foot.
Six scientists stood in a storm.
Seven scary saxophones sung a song.
Eight eyes ate the enemy.
Nine noble nuns knitted a knife.
Ten tarty tarantulas talked for ten years.

Annie Appleton (9)
The Grey House School

SNOW

Snow is not forever like a friend,
But like ice melting in the sun,
White like the clouds,
Glimmering and glittering.

The little paws of cats and dogs,
Leaving a trail of footprints there and back,
Children having snowball fights,
And making snowmen!

Rebecca Fisher (9)
The Grey House School

I AM ME

I am in my own world, always dreaming
I am interested in everything
I am a car fanatic
I am me.

I am always collecting things, always more
I am like 007
I am never the same
I am me.

I am like the stars, always shining
I am like the planets
I am like Monsters Inc
I am me.

I am in my own world
I am interested in everything
I am a car fanatic
I am me.

Jack MacNally (9)
Westbourne Primary School

ALL ALONE

I like to be alone,
Nobody there,
Behind the sofa,
I don't care.

And then he comes,
Quiet as a mouse,
No movement at all,
In the house.

I like to be alone,
No noise around,
Everyone's quiet,
Me not found.

And then he comes,
Quiet as a mouse,
No noise at all,
In the house.

I like to be alone,
No nosy mums,
Then I say softly,
'Come, come, come.'

And then he comes,
Quiet as a mouse,
No movement at all,
In the house.

I'm not really alone,
When mousie's here,
I'm not really alone,
When mousie's near.

Emily Davies (8)
Westbourne Primary School

THE UNIVERSE

Infinity
Crimson ball of gas and fire
Never-ending, it's a promise
A place where stars hide to be happy
Undiscovered - not there?
Extraordinary - not there
Extraordinary dreams
Lost dreams
The universe

Alone
Weird, strange beings
Space-hopping amongst planets
The crimson planet, Mars
Star-filled place of Heaven
Above us all
Alone

Imaginary
The place of dreams
No cares
Black holes - not there?
The fire ball
Is anyone out there?

James Harrison (8)
Westbourne Primary School

ALONE

When I am alone I like to
Toy with my playhouse
Play with my toy mouse
Say hello to a passer-by wood louse

When I am by myself I like to
Go to a secret place
Way above space
Everything there is ace

But when I am with dreamless creatures
My head and thoughts displaced
For all my thoughts encased
For my thoughts must now escape.

Hannah Jones (8)
Westbourne Primary School

SNOW IS SNOW

Let the icy river flow, flow, flow.
It doesn't matter if you don't have any money,
people laugh and make it funny.
Wishes never come true for you.
The time goes fast,
hear the blackbirds go past.
Here in school I have lots of friends,
in my drawer I have lots of pens.
My own world, everything is alive,
my sister likes to dive.
My brother likes snow,
and my brother runs and says, 'No, no, no.'

Thomas Drinkwater (8)
Westbourne Primary School

MY FAMILY

Happy, cosy home
With my family
Mum, Dad, little sister
And goldfish too
That's my family

Roast dinners on Sunday
With my family
Holidays in France
Playing pool together
That's my family

EastEnders on TV
With my family
Disneyland in Paris
Happy times together
That's my family.

Michaela Hamilton (8)
Westbourne Primary School

UNICORNS

A glittering, shimmering field of diamonds,
His long mane flowing like a waterfall of silver.
A glittering, shimmering field of diamonds,
His hooves spray golden stars as he runs like the wind.

Unicorns, unicorns
Sparkling horn of crystal.
Unicorns, unicorns
Rearing to the stars.

Lucie Olive-Jones (9)
Westbourne Primary School

MY DOG

My dog is my best friend
part of our family
but special to me
my dog hears my secrets
she keeps them too
never tells anyone

My dog is five years old
part of our family
but special to me
a King Charles cavalier
full of hugs and fun
Meg is the best.

Jemma Barlow (9)
Westbourne Primary School

MY TREE

My tree is as peaceful
as a bird in the sky
frothed with snow in winter
lifting me up high

My tree stands as still
as a statue made of stone
always there for me
whenever I'm alone.

My tree feels as gentle
as a feather on the breeze
rough and smooth together
my friend, the whole world sees.

Aaron Smith (9)
Westbourne Primary School

MY ALIEN

One day an alien came down
Came down from outer space
From outer space he came and started to sing
The song he sang, it goes like this . . .

'I am a little, little alien
And I come from out of space
And I sing what can I sing
The alien song, the alien song
The alien song, the alien song.
I shall sing the alien song
And that's quite right.'

I said, 'I've never seen an alien before.'
So that's my poem
Alright?

Shannon Hamilton (8)
Westbourne Primary School

SPACE

Space is a never-ending silly race,
It is silence leaking from cupped hands,
Like ice-cold mountain water.

The sun is hot but space is cold.
We are fine, like bees in their own hive.

Bradley Shepherd (9)
Westbourne Primary School

ALL IN THE MIND

Peace is like a butterfly
soft-winged
like snowflake.

Hand like ice-cold
mountain water
flowing on the rocks.

Peace is the wind
blowing on the trees
swishing all day long.

Looking at the rainbow
after the storm.

Rosie Johnson (9)
Westbourne Primary School

THE FOOTBALL GROUND

I love the way they play
On the football ground
I cannot understand
The words
It's too fast for me
I get confused
I'm happy when they win
When they lose I'm sad.

Kevin Treagus (8)
Westbourne Primary School

EXPERIENCE IN SPACE

Going up to space
Leaving Earth's atmosphere
My first time
The building fear
I remember the shuttle.

I hear a *creak*
I hear a *crack*
I gaze from the window
I see only tiny Earth, like a golf ball in the black.

Now trembling with dismay
A fragment flies off
A small piece of nose cone
I check the monitor
All fine.

Now sweating with dread
Just want to go home
But no choice.

Close to a planet
I know we are safe now
We land. Phew!

Joseph Dyer (9)
Westbourne Primary School

MY SCHOOL

My school means friendship,
My school means work,
But fun too.
My school is happy,
My school is beautiful,
And friendly too.
My school is play times,
My school means games,
And learning too.

Billy Ayres (8)
Westbourne Primary School

FROSTY TIMES

F   rosty weather means winter weather and that's what I like this year,
R   aindrops fall and form into icicles so sharp I shiver with fear,
O   ver the hill the sun goes down and the night comes into full bloom,
S   now is falling, winter is here, I am warm from the heat in my room,
T   winkling snowflakes fall outside and snow is everywhere,
Y   esterday I had fun but still cold, but now I can't think of a care.

T   omorrow has come, the sun is shining making the world reappear,
I   n the outside world somewhere it is hot but I know it is cold
                                            around here,
M   e and my friends play out in the air and we make sure we
                                            are wrapped up warm,
E   verywhere is perfect as if it has been drawn,
S   o that's what this winter is like.

Charlotte Newman (9)
Whitewater CE Primary School

FROSTY DAYS

Outside the bitter wind is blowing,
Icicles dangling down from the roof,
Christmas trees smelling of the outside,
Pavements piled in white crunching snow.

Fires burning, stars twinkling,
Trees covered in snow, leaves freezing,
Ready to drift down under the snow,
Pavements piled in white crunching snow.

Animals are snuggled up for the winter,
Everything is still and calm,
Jack Frost coming around,
Pavements piled in white crunching snow.

Charlotte Baker (9)
Whitewater CE Primary School

CHRISTMAS TIME

Sledging down the side of a hill is so much fun,
Sitting by the fire eating a toasted bun;
Having snowball fights is so good,
Sitting at the table, eating Christmas pud!
Waking up at 3 o'clock in the morning,
Opening my presents when I'm yawning.
Remembering Jesus born in a shed,
When he was resting his poor little head.
Father Christmas riding his sledge.
I love Christmas!

Jack Mitchell (8)
Whitewater CE Primary School

CHRISTMASTIME

C hrist the Lord was born,
H appy children play,
R oast dinners are cooking,
I gloos fall down,
S ongs are sung
T roubles are forgotten,
M erry carols are played,
A nd Santa leaves you presents.
S easons have changed.

Max Davies (8)
Whitewater CE Primary School

CHRISTMAS

C hristmas cake in the oven,
H appy smiles on my face,
R ustling of Christmas paper,
I cing the Christmas cake.
S ome delicious smells waft from the kitchen,
T asting them is always the best!
M easure the pile of presents on the doorstep,
A lovely new toy soldier from
S anta Claus and lots of other toys too.

Dominique Cooper (7)
Whitewater CE Primary School

FIREWORKS

I love fireworks, they shine on me.
I love fireworks, they sparkle on me.
I like fireworks, they go *bang* by me!
They are very pretty, just like me . . .

Hannah Cutler (7)
Whitewater CE Primary School

SNOW

Snow falls softly, going all ways
like white leaves sparkling,
floating down onto the snowy grass.
Snow is water and melts when it falls on to you.
It melts and disappears.

Connor Gains (7)
Whitewater CE Primary School

SNOW IS . . .

Different shapes and sizes,
Soft cotton wool balls being thrown,
Like a blanket falling from the sky to the ground,
Beautiful flakes melting in my hand,
Like tickly feathers drifting calmly to the floor,
Fairies fluttering down to the wet, shiny surface,
Time to wrap up warm.

Jessica Vickery (8)
Whitewater CE Primary School

WHAT AM I?

I run across the snowy ground,
Looking for the tastiest acorns.
I shall soon have to hibernate.

My browny fur keeping me warm,
I judge how far I have to jump to get to that tree.
I shall soon have to hibernate.

I keep watch for a human,
Here comes one now.
Now is the time to hibernate.

As I climb up the tree,
Jumping here and there,
I think, *did I collect enough acorns?*
Now I am hibernating.

Richard Nutton (10)
Whitewater CE Primary School

SNOWFLAKES

Snowflakes are sparkly, soft and wet,
Snowflakes secretly fall on your head,
They are like fairies fluttering by,
Snowflakes are coming down from the sky,
Snowflakes remind me of fun,
I love snowflakes, they look like cotton wool on me,
They carry my dreams all around,
They take my wishes up to God.

I love snowflakes!

Alice Cresswell (8)
Whitewater CE Primary School

MY AUTUMN POEM

Hedgehogs hibernating under green and golden leaves,
Badgers coming out of their big dark setts.
Squirrels scurrying and running up trees,
Autumn is a time when children like to play.

Conkers falling from the trees,
Children playing conker fighting.
Rain trickling over our heads,
We stay at home in front of the big orange flames.

Acorns falling everywhere,
Animals don't seem to bother or care.
They hibernate all snug and warm,
Until the sun comes next year.

Tiffany Mason (10)
Whitewater CE Primary School

THE RABBIT

Noses twitching in the morning air
They see me coming, stop and stare
Whiskers glistening in the sun
All of a sudden off they run
Stopping to look, standing high
Ears pointing to the sky
Down the burrow one, two, three
The warren must be under the tree.

Rebecca Mark (9)
Whitewater CE Primary School

WINTER VACATION

It's bitterly cold and nippy,
My friend Winter is getting a bit hippy
Arctic cold is taking over
Tomorrow I'm going in a warm Land Rover.

Finally it's come, it's finally here
I'm so close, I'm so near
To watching the glittery dance of snow
My hair sways as the wind blows.

Rhys Higgs (9)
Whitewater CE Primary School

GUESS WHO?

Loud snorer
Long sleeper
Ham eater
Foot heater
Leaf chaser
Sweet player
Loud purrer
Fluff maker
Bird catcher
Tree scratcher
Garden digger
Tail tickler.

Emily Blunden (11)
Whitewater CE Primary School

WINTER

As I cannot wait to
Go on a ski lift
As I cannot wait to
Learn to ski
As I cannot wait to
See the view
Up high in a
Mountain
As I cannot wait to
See all the wonderful
Things like snow
Falling
Down
Down
And hitting the ground
With my dad hoping
I will not fall and break
My back!
And I cannot wait

For you to come too!

Alex Brooks (9)
Whitewater CE Primary School

SNOW

Calmly drifting like droplets of cloud
Like a feather tickling but softly
It's like a blanket covering the world, making it stop
Fluffy, wet and cold like cotton wool but silent
That's my *snow.*

Nancy Scally (7)
Whitewater CE Primary School

WHAT AM I?

Joke maker
Pie hater
Laughter provider
Unicycle rider
Water sprayer
Accordion player
Super juggler
Tightrope struggler
Key factor . . .
. . . Circus actor!

Lily Cresswell (10)
Whitewater CE Primary School

SNOW

Snow makes me feel fresh and happy.
The ground is like a carpet of snow.
It drifts silently down, like a mouse
Tiptoeing across the floorboards.
It is cold, wet, white, gentle and pretty.
It feels like cotton wool.
It tickles me, my nose goes bright red!
It falls gently on my jumper and lies around my feet.

Florence Perry (7)
Whitewater CE Primary School

FIREWORKS

'Fireworks, fireworks,' everyone said the day we went to bonfire night.
Everyone was mad with delight!
Fireworks went *bang, smash.*
They're beautiful like little roses in the air.
I'm in bed asleep at night with my little teddy.
We hear the fireworks sparkle, crackle and *whizz,*
Like the moon's falling from the night sky.

Siân Nabbs (8)
Whitewater CE Primary School

SLUGGO

Pro skater
Ramp flier
Rail grinder
Street skater
World rider
Comp skater
Goofy skater.

Jonathan McMillan (10)
Whitewater CE Primary School

GUESS WHO?

Cheeky walker
Loud talker
Nasty tricker
Zoo hater
Banana lover
Tree swinger.

Amy Cutler (11)
Whitewater CE Primary School

KILLER WHALE

The black and white whale arches its back
And leaps out of the water
Then plunges back into the water again
Nearly skimming the bottom.
Its calf, trying to follow her, does a bellyflop,
Then ends up showing his white belly before he lands.

Nearby seals are swimming,
Not knowing the danger they are in,
Then breaking the surface of the water,
Her calf, shortly behind, grabs a seal and they swim off.

Helena Clough (9)
Whitewater CE Primary School

TIGER

Great stalker,
strong walker,
powerful striker,
amazing hiker,
loud roarer,
rare mauler,
Indian breeder,
animal leader,
dangerous leaper,
striped sleeper.

Joshua Aldridge (10)
Whitewater CE Primary School

THE DOLPHIN

See the dolphins jumping,
Flying through the air.
Light, sky-blue skin,
Sliding across the ocean.
Smooth, wet skin
Diving under the water,
Playing hide-and-seek.
Men with nets,
Hunting dolphins.
But they are too quick,
Racing along the sea
Like deer.
Oh so beautiful,
So graceful.

Orla King (9)
Whitewater CE Primary School

LION KENNING

Loud roarer
Quiet snorer
Animal killer
Blood chiller
Mane wearer
People scarer
Flesh eater
Life cheater.

Robert Towse (10)
Whitewater CE Primary School

FIREWORKS

Fireworks *whizzing* in the black, clear night sky.
Popping, banging, crackling sounds all around.
Boys and girls playing with their pretty sparklers,
making lots of wonderful shapes.
The loud *bang* of the shooting, brightly coloured rockets
and the colourful flames of the huge, hot bonfire.
The guy on the bonfire is burning away
bursting into flames!
There are so many wonderful colours all around us,
I love Bonfire Night.

Robert Mandry (8)
Whitewater CE Primary School

SNAKE

Snake slithers
through the
grass with a
hissing sound.
It makes its way
like a glider.
It's greenish
body in the
grass, hiding
from the sun.

Benjamin Milloritt (9)
Whitewater CE Primary School

OWL

Wise old owl
Silently surveying
Head turned
Upside down
Looking, searching, watching.
Hunters coming!
Quick, hide!
Looking, searching, watching.
Time for bed
Hard night
Looking, searching, watching.

Edward Blunden (9)
Whitewater CE Primary School

EVIL KNIEVIL

United States dweller
Big seller
Motorbike rider
Stunt striver
High flier
Daredevil trier
Truck leaper
Record keeper
Injury taker
History maker.

Miles Hope (11)
Whitewater CE Primary School

GUESS WHO?

A large, brown lump dosing under the sun's gaze.
Slowly he heaves his great body up and has a long, hard sniff.
Then he grunts to himself and walks forward one, two, three steps.
He takes another sniff, he can smell his home.
He begins to drag his large body towards his burrow.
Just before he goes into his home he spies a patch of food.
He grabs it with his teeth and takes it home for him and his family.

Kerry Corley (9)
Whitewater CE Primary School

ME, TREE

As the wind rushes through me
As my leaves shudder with coldness
Falling off to the bottom of the world
As I look down at children playing and eating
Someone is coming to water me, feed me
As I look down with glee
I just stay here listening to see if the wind rushes past me.

Harriet Croft (9)
Whitewater CE Primary School

GUESS WHO?

Cheese eater,
Hole sneaker,
Beady peeper,
Elephant scarer,
Cat hater!

Rebecca Green
Whitewater CE Primary School

My Dog 'Yeti'

Thunder hater
Slobbery licker
Ball racer
Tongue swinger
Hungry eater
Ear pointer
Nose sniffer
Tail wagger
Walk lover
Stick fetcher
Cat chaser!

Rebecca Bulmer (10)
Whitewater CE Primary School

Kenning

Good skater
TV watcher
Food eater
Champion skater
900 lander
Music listener
Birdhouse skater
Hawk wearer

Tony Hawk.

Jack Dingley (10)
Whitewater CE Primary School